First World War
and Army of Occupation
War Diary
France, Belgium and Germany

GUARDS DIVISION
1 Guards Brigade
Headquarters
1 October 1916 - 30 November 1916

WO95/1213/2

The Naval & Military Press Ltd
www.nmarchive.com
Published in association with The National Archives

Published by

The Naval & Military Press Ltd

Unit 10 Ridgewood Industrial Park,

Uckfield, East Sussex,

TN22 5QE England

Tel: +44 (0) 1825 749494

www.naval-military-press.com

www.nmarchive.com

This diary has been reprinted in facsimile from the original. Any imperfections are inevitably reproduced and the quality may fall short of modern type and cartographic standards.

© **Crown Copyright**
Images reproduced by permission of The National Archives, London, England, 2015.

Contents

Document type	Place/Title	Date From	Date To
Heading	WO95/1213 Oct 1916.		
War Diary	Morlancourt To Dromesnil.	01/10/1916	01/10/1916
War Diary	Dromesnil	02/10/1916	31/10/1916
Miscellaneous	Apps. 242. Apps 239 240 241 Missing.		
Operation(al) Order(s)	1st Guards Brigade Order No. 84.	30/10/1916	30/10/1916
Miscellaneous	March Table.		
Miscellaneous	Headquarters, Guards Division.	31/10/1916	31/10/1916
Heading	War Diary B.H.Q. 1st Guards Brigade November 1916.		
War Diary	Dromesnil.	01/11/1916	11/11/1916
War Diary	Citadel F.21.6.	12/10/1916	12/10/1916
War Diary	S.24.b.4.9.	13/11/1916	21/11/1916
War Diary	S.23.b.4.9. To Sandpits Camp. E.24.d.	22/11/1916	30/11/1916
Heading	Divisional Operation Orders		
Miscellaneous	G.D. No. 2345/G.	04/11/1916	04/11/1916
Miscellaneous	Warning Order.	06/11/1916	06/11/1916
Operation(al) Order(s)	Guards Division Order No. 88.	07/11/1916	07/11/1916
Miscellaneous	March Table For Movement Of Transport And Mounted Units, Issued With Guards Division Order No. 88.		
Operation(al) Order(s)	Amendment To Guards Division Order No. 88.	07/11/1916	07/11/1916
Miscellaneous	Amended March Table For Movement Of Transport And Mounted Units, Issued With Guards Division Order No. 88.		
Operation(al) Order(s)	Guards Division Order No. 89.	09/11/1916	09/11/1916
Miscellaneous			
Operation(al) Order(s)	Guards Division Order No. 90.	09/11/1916	09/11/1916
Operation(al) Order(s)	Guards Division Order No. 91.	09/11/1916	09/11/1916
Miscellaneous	Appendix To Accompany Guards Division Order No. 91.		
Operation(al) Order(s)	Guards Division Order No. 92.	11/11/1916	11/11/1916
Miscellaneous			
Operation(al) Order(s)	Guards Division Order No. 93.	15/11/1916	15/11/1916
Miscellaneous	G.D. No. 2473/G.	13/11/1916	13/11/1916
Operation(al) Order(s)	Warning Order. Guards Division Order No. 94.	16/11/1916	16/11/1916
Operation(al) Order(s)	Amendment To Guards Division Order No. 94.	16/11/1916	16/11/1916
Operation(al) Order(s)	Guards Division Order No: 95.	18/11/1916	18/11/1916
Miscellaneous	Movements Of Guards Brigade During Relief. Appendix "A".		
Miscellaneous	Distribution On Completion Of Relief. Appendix "B".		
Miscellaneous	Movements Of 5th Australian Division As For As It Affects Guards Division. Appendix "C".		
Operation(al) Order(s)	Warning Order. Guards Division Order No. 96.	25/11/1916	25/11/1916
Miscellaneous	C Form (Duplicate). Messages And Signals.		
Operation(al) Order(s)	Warning Order. Guards Division Order No: 97.	26/11/1916	26/11/1916
Operation(al) Order(s)	Guards Division Order No. 100.	05/12/1916	05/12/1916
Miscellaneous	G.D. No. 2561/G.	30/11/1916	30/11/1916
Miscellaneous			
Operation(al) Order(s)	Guards Division Order No. 99.	29/11/1916	29/11/1916
Miscellaneous	C Form (Duplicate). Messages And Signals.		
Operation(al) Order(s)	Guards Division Order No. 98.	29/11/1916	29/11/1916

Type	Description	Date	Date
Heading	Brigade Operation Orders		
Operation(al) Order(s)	1st Guards Brigade Order No. 85.	31/10/1916	31/10/1916
Miscellaneous	March Table		
Operation(al) Order(s)	1st Guards Brigade Order No. 86.	07/11/1916	07/11/1916
Miscellaneous	2nd Bn. Grenadier Guards.	02/11/1916	02/11/1916
Miscellaneous	March Table	10/11/1916	10/11/1916
Operation(al) Order(s)	1st Guards Brigade Order No. 87.	09/11/1916	09/11/1916
Miscellaneous	March Table		
Operation(al) Order(s)	1st Guards Brigade Order No. 88.	09/11/1916	09/11/1916
Miscellaneous	Movement Table.		
Operation(al) Order(s)	Supplement to 1st Guards Brigade Order No. 88.	11/11/1916	11/11/1916
Miscellaneous	Movement Table.		
Operation(al) Order(s)	1st Guards Brigade Order No. 89.	15/11/1916	15/11/1916
Operation(al) Order(s)	Supplement to 1st Guards Brigade Order No. 89.	16/11/1916	16/11/1916
Operation(al) Order(s)	Supplement to 1st Guards Bde., Order No. 89.	17/11/1916	17/11/1916
Map	Map Y.19.		
Operation(al) Order(s)	Warning Order. 1st Guards Brigade Order No. 90.	16/11/1916	16/11/1916
Operation(al) Order(s)	1st Guards Brigade Order No. 91.	18/11/1916	18/11/1916
Miscellaneous	Movements Of Guards Brigades During Relief. Appendix "A".		
Miscellaneous	Distribution Of Completion Of Relief. Appendix "B".		
Miscellaneous	2nd Bn. Grenadier Guards.	12/11/1916	12/11/1916
Miscellaneous	Any Units not shown in following Tables march under Brigade arrangements in accordance with Guards Division Order No. 95 (Appendix A)		
Operation(al) Order(s)	Supplement to 1st Guards Bde. Order No. 91.	19/11/1916	19/11/1916
Miscellaneous	1st G.B. No. 523/5.	20/11/1916	20/11/1916
Miscellaneous	Instructions "RE" Work Platoons Re-Joining Their Battalions.		
Operation(al) Order(s)	Warning Order 1st Guards Brigade Order No. 92.	25/11/1916	25/11/1916
Heading	2nd Guards Brigade Operation Orders		
Operation(al) Order(s)	Operation Order No. 77 By Brigadier-General Lord H.C. Seymour, D.S.O. Commanding 2nd. Guards Brigade.	27/11/1916	27/11/1916
Heading	Defence Scheme Scheme Of Work Roster Of Reliefs Handing Over Notes		
Miscellaneous	1st G.B. No. 523/4.	17/11/1916	17/11/1916
Miscellaneous	Defence Scheme For Right Group Of Guards Division.	17/11/1916	17/11/1916
Miscellaneous	General Scheme of Work in Right Group of Guards Division.	15/11/1916	15/11/1916
Miscellaneous	2nd Bn. Grenadier Guards.	12/11/1916	12/11/1916
Miscellaneous	1st G.B. No. 501.	15/11/1916	15/11/1916
Miscellaneous	Position and Comments Of Right Group Battalions Of Guards Division.		
Miscellaneous	Handing Over Notes On 1st Guards Brigade Sector.	20/11/1916	20/11/1916
Heading	Intelligence		
Miscellaneous	Intelligence Report.	18/11/1916	18/11/1916
Miscellaneous	Intelligence Report.	16/11/1916	16/11/1916

WO 95
1213
OCT 1916

WAR DIARY or **INTELLIGENCE SUMMARY**

Army Form C. 2118.

October 1915

Vol 15

HEADQUARTERS 2 - NOV 1916 1st GUARDS BRIGADE

Place	Date	Hour	Summary of Events and Information	Remarks and references to Appendices
MORLANCOURT to DROMESNIL	Oct 2nd	1 am	All watches put back 1 hour.	
		9.40 am	The Bde moved off as per 1st Gds Bde order No 83 to busses for bus area. All arrangements for this were made & carried out by the French. There was awful accommodation to only one bus broken down. The entrainment was carried out well & quickly — all roads kept past an officer she counted them — going every 30 seconds also took there 30 strength to his bus. On arrival of the Bde was distributed as follows: Bde HQ. DROMESNIL 3rd Coldm Gds SELINCOURT 75th Coy R.E. VILLERS 2nd Gren Gds AUMONT 1st Irish Gds HORNOY 4th F.A " 2nd Coldm Gds DROMESNIL 2 Gds Coy & T.M.By. HORNOY 3 Coy Thain BOISRAULT	APP 239
DROMESNIL	Oct 3rd		Weather wet — training impossible —	
"	Oct 4th		Conference of Officers commanding Grenadier & Coldstream Bns at Div H.Q. Rained most of the day. The Brigade Major proceeded on leave to England. Very little training possible.	

Army Form C. 2118.

WAR DIARY
or
INTELLIGENCE SUMMARY
(Erase heading not required.)

Instructions regarding War Diaries and Intelligence Summaries are contained in F. S. Regs, Part II. and the Staff Manual respectively. Title Pages will be prepared in manuscript.

Place	Date	Hour	Summary of Events and Information	Remarks and references to Appendices
BROMESNIL	Oct. 5th		Major General presented medal ribbons to Battalions of the Brigade starting with 2nd Bn. Cold Gds. Proceeding to 3rd Bn Cold Gds. 1st Bn Irish Gds. Bde M.G. Coy. 2nd Bn Gren Gds. Meeting at Div HQrs of Brigadiers by the Army Commander.	
"	Oct. 6th		Battalions drilling and route marching. Weather fine	
"	Oct. 7th		In Billets. Elementary training. Weather fine	
"	Oct. 8th		Church parades by all Battalions in their billets. Rain in the morning	
"	Oct. 9th		In Billets. Training. Fine.	
"	Oct. 10th		Billets	
"	Oct. 11th	10.30 a.m.	Conference of Commanding Officers at Brigade HQrs	
"	Oct. 12th		Billets. Weather fine.	
"	Oct. 13th		Billets	

Army Form C. 2118.

WAR DIARY
or
INTELLIGENCE SUMMARY
(Erase heading not required.)

Instructions regarding War Diaries and Intelligence Summaries are contained in F. S. Regs., Part II. and the Staff Manual respectively. Title Pages will be prepared in manuscript.

Place	Date	Hour	Summary of Events and Information	Remarks and references to Appendices
DROMESNIL	Oct 14th		Battalions carried out simple schemes on Advanced Guards and Outposts. Weather fair.	
"	Oct 15th	10am	G.D. No. 238g/25 received ordering Bde Div to move on 19 - 20 - 21st. Church parades for all units. Weather very showery.	App. 240
"	Oct 16th	2pm	Bde Major returned from leave - Staff Captain proceeded on leave Order for Div to move on 19-20-21 cancelled.	App. 241
"	Oct 17th		Weather wet & little training possible -	
"	Oct 18th to 21st		The weather during remainder of week was fine & training in Bde Ryfl[?] Bns was carried on — with a view to carrying out Bn training later on — The courses for the training of bombing instructors in Bns were brought to a close - 2 Officers & 16 N.C.Os per Bn. having been trained — The eighteen & further 100 coys a day through a four hour course was started again - The Major General proceeded on leave & the Brigadier took over command of the Div but remained at Bde H.Q.	

WAR DIARY
or
INTELLIGENCE SUMMARY

Army Form C. 2118.

Place	Date	Hour	Summary of Events and Information	Remarks and references to Appendices
BROMESNIL	Oct 21st to Oct 29th		During this week the weather again considerably interfered with training but the instruction in open warfare was carried on - simple Tactical schemes were carried out by Coy Commanders under the Bn Major. On Oct 26th Brig Gen. Pereira proceeded on leave - On Oct 27th London Gazette announced that Lt Col G.V. Campbell 2nd Coy 2nd Bn Coldstream Gds had been awarded the Victoria Cross. During the latter part of the week Bdes were warned that H.R.H. The Duke of Connaught would inspect the Bde on 4 Nov, and Battns had to be worked out -	APP 242
Oct 31st			Divisional rehearsal for Parade by H.R.H. The Duke of Connaught -	

J. Campbell
Lt. Col.
Commg 1st Gds Bde.

aff 242

affs 239
240
241

missing

Copy No.

242

1st Guards Brigade Order No. 84.

Ref. Map - DIEPPE 1/100,000.   October 30th, 1916.

1.   The Brigade will parade to-morrow, October 31st, for
        a Divisional Rehearsal of the Review of the Guards
        Division by H. R. H. The Duke of Connaught.

2.   March Table is attached.

3.   Dress :- Will be the same as that laid down in para. 8
        of the Divisional Orders issued yesterday.

4.   Sgt. Majors and one (right) marker for each half Company
        of Battalions and Machine Gun Company, and a right marker
        for Trench Mortar Battery will report to Brigade Major at
        DROMESNIL Windmill at 8-45 A.M.
        2nd Bn. Grenadier Guards will detail a (right) marker for
        the Medal men of the Brigade to report to the senior Sgt.
        Major near the flagstaff as soon as possible after H. R. H.
        has passed the Battalion.

        ACKNOWLEDGE.

                                                Captain,
                                Brigade Major, 1st Guards Brigade.

Issued through Signals at :-

Copy No. 1   2nd Bn. Grenadier Guards.
         2   2nd Bn. Coldstream Guards.
         3   3rd Bn. Coldstream Guards.
         4   1st Bn. Irish Guards.
         5   Bde., Machine Gun Company.
         6   1st Guards T. M. Battery.
         7   Staff Captain.
         8   Guards Division.
         9 & 10 Retained.

1.

MARCH TABLE.

Order of March.	Route.	Starting Point.	Time.	Remarks.
3/Cold.Gds.	SELINCOURT - DROMESNIL Road.	Road Junction 400 yds. N.W. of D of DROMESNIL.	10-5 A.M.	To keep clear of main Street in DROMESNIL.
2/Cold.Gds.	Direct.	"	10-9 A.M.	
1/Irish Gds.	HORNOY - BOIS-RAULT - O of B. de la CORROYE.	"	10-13 A.M.	
2/Gren.Gds.	AUMONT - SELINCOURT.	"	10-17 A.M.	Not to enter SELINCOURT until 3/Cold.Gds. are clear.
Bde.M.G.Coy.) T.M.Battery.)	As for 1/Irish Gds.	"	10-21 A.M.	Machine Gun Company will parade with Gun Limbers.

N.B.

(a) All Troops of the Brigade will move South of the BELLOY - VILLERS - to the parade ground keeping clear of the Road.

(b) Battalions will move on their markers from the right passing by the S.E. corner of the parade ground, and will form up on their markers facing right in Quarter Column of half Coy's.

(c) Bde., M.G. Company and T. M. Battery will halt on the S. side of the BELLOY - VILLERS Road opposite their markers - as soon as 2nd Guards Brigade have passed down this Road they will move straight on their markers.

243/A.

#15
31/10/16

Headquarters,

Guards Division.

Reference your A.B. 267 of to-day's date.

Herewith Field States as requested -

2nd Bn. Grenadier Guards.

Officer Commanding - Lieut-Col., C.R.C. de Crespigny, D.S.

Officers   -   25.
Other Ranks -   787.

2nd Bn. Coldstream Guards.

Officer Commanding - Lt-Col., R.B.J. Crawfurd, D.S.O.

Officers   -   21.
Other Ranks -   670.

3rd Bn. Coldstream Guards.

Officer Commanding - Major F. Longueville,

Officers   -   17.
Other Ranks -   698.

1st Bn. Irish Guards.

Officer Commanding - Lt-Col., R.C.A. McCalmont.

Officers   -   19.
Other Ranks -   719.

Bde. Machine Gun Company.

Officer Commanding - Captain R.C. Bingham.

Officers   -   10.
Other Ranks -
    (Establishment) 173.
    (attached)   82.

1st Guards T. M. Battery.

Officer Commanding - T.W.A. Earle.

Officers   -   3.
Other Ranks -   49.

31st October 1916.

Lieut-Colonel,
Commdg., 1st Guards Brigade.

WAR DIARY

B. H. Q.

1st Guards Brigade

November 1916

Army Form C. 2118

WAR DIARY
or
INTELLIGENCE SUMMARY
(Erase heading not required.)

HQ 1st Guards Bde
1.11.16.
Vol 16

Place	Date	Hour	Summary of Events and Information	Remarks and references to Appendices
MOMESNIL	Nov 12th	11.15am	The Div was inspected by H.R.H. the Duke of Connaught. After riding along in front & in rear of the Division H.R.H. addressed all Officers - W.C.O.s & men who had received decorations during the war. He expressed his pleasure at the appearance of the Division on parade. After the parade was over the units marched past the Duke in fours on their way back to billets.	APP 243
	Nov 3rd	1 pm	Tactical schemes carried out with Coy commanders of 2nd & 3rd Coldstream. Orders received to send one Bn. up to front line area for pioneer work - 2nd Coldstream detailed.	APP 244
	Nov 5th	9 am	Church services as usual - 1st Line Transport 2nd Coldstream left by road -	
	Nov 6th	7.30am	2nd Coldstream left in busses for XIV Corps area -	
	Nov 7th	9 am	1st Div Warning Order received to be ready to move up into XIV Corps area on 10th or 11th Nov. received - & a message sent to all units warning them of the same -	APP 245

WAR DIARY or INTELLIGENCE SUMMARY

Army Form C. 2118.

Place	Date	Hour	Summary of Events and Information	Remarks and references to Appendices
DROMESNIL	Nov 7th	2 pm	Wire to confirm by wire that 1st Div. Transport would move the following day.	APP 248
		5 pm	5th Div. Orders No 88 received	APP 249
		7.30 pm	1st Div. Order No 86 issued	
	Nov 8th		1st Div. Transport moved into XIV Corps area	
		9.30 am	5th Div. Orders No 89 received	APP 248
		2 pm	5th Div. Order No 87 issued	" 249
		8 pm	5th Div. Order No 91 received	" 250
		9 pm	5th Div. Order No 88 issued	" 251
	Nov 10th	10 am	By this hour the personnel of the Bde were embarked in accordance with 1st D.R Order No 87. The buses were supplied by the French. The journey was well executed & the Bde was all in the CITADEL camp by 7.30 pm. This camp was most uncomfortable & a day in mud	
	Nov 11th		3rd C.D.btrys & 5th moved w.t to A. camp = TRONES WOOD. & 7.Siege Bdes & Bde Ad. 5/2 to F. camp = MONTAUBAN	APP. 252
		4 pm 6.30 pm	5th Div. Order No 92 received. 1st Bde Supplement to Order No 88 issued	APP 253

WAR DIARY or INTELLIGENCE SUMMARY

Army Form C. 2118.

(Erase heading not required.)

Instructions regarding War Diaries and Intelligence Summaries are contained in F.S. Regs., Part II. and the Staff Manual respectively. Title Pages will be prepared in manuscript.

Place	Date	Hour	Summary of Events and Information	Remarks and references to Appendices
CITADEL T.21.b.	Nov 12th		2nd Grenadier Gds moved to X Camp Montauban. 3rd Coldstream Gds moved into X sector of new Bde front taking over from 7th East Yorks & 7th Yorkshire Regiment.	
		2.30 p.m.	Conference of Brigadiers at 3rd Gds Bde H.Q. about new line.	
	Nov 13th	Noon	Bde H.Q. moved to just East of WATERLOT Farm — taking over from so called 1st Irish Gds moved into Left subsector taking over from Left Half of 7th Yorks & 8th South Staffords — O.R. Bde 2.D.5, 1 K. 2 W. Casualties 2nd C.G. 2 K. 3 W. O.R. 3rd C.G. 2 K. 4 W. 2nd Lt T.F. POWELL wounded. During the day there was considerable shelling	
S.24.b.4.9	Nov 14th	4 a.m.	Situation normal — The front this am was left comparatively quiet & all over the Bde sector — The hostile shelling little damage was done by the Bde was from N.34.c.7.1 to N.29 central. The front taken over by the Bde was deep & in poor condition but there was no communication to it	

WAR DIARY
INTELLIGENCE SUMMARY
(Erase heading not required.)

Army Form C. 2118.

Place	Date	Hour	Summary of Events and Information	Remarks and references to Appendices
S.27.d.4.9		20 N	by day. In fact there were no communication trenches in any of the line with the result that there was much too much movement across the open by day. This attracted hostile shelling which was continuous. A lot of "Duck Boards" led to Coy. Bn. H.Q. + if this all relies + carrying parties had to pass. Rations + water carrying was done entirely by mules transport - mules being digged for this purpose. Casualties 3rd C.P. D.R. 2.K. G.W. 1st O.R. 2 O.R. 2 wounded. Weather hot and became very cold but strong wind was counted. Was needed to devote all energies to making a good front + support line + getting communication up to it. Pressure from Bn. on to Coy also taken in hand - the difficulty by still was to get up sufficient returns + there was a lack of trench boards — During night hours 18/13 & 3rd Coy relieved 3rd Coy Labs. Casualties 2 C.B. O.R. 1.S.B. I.W. 1K. 1W. 1M. 2nd R.Coy - 3W.	

Army Form C. 2118.

WAR DIARY
or
INTELLIGENCE SUMMARY
(Erase heading not required.)

Instructions regarding War Diaries and Intelligence Summaries are contained in F. S. Regs., Part II. and the Staff Manual respectively. Title Pages will be prepared in manuscript.

Place	Date	Hour	Summary of Events and Information	Remarks and references to Appendices
S.24.b.4.9	Nov 16th	4 am	Situation normal - Enemy again shelled forward area continuously during the night.	
		12 noon	Casualties 2nd Cold. Gds. Lt. S. O. CROMBIE wounded.	
			3rd Cold. Gds. 13 O.R. wounded. 1 O.R. missing	
			1st Irish Gds. 4 O.R. "	A/L 205
		2 pm	Order warning Bde that it would be relieved on 21/22 received	
		4 pm	Situation normal - nothing to report	
		6 pm	1st Gds. Bde. order No 90 warning Bde about relief.	205
		8 pm	Defence scheme issued -	207
			2nd Irish Gds. relieved 1st Irish Gds. in left sector -	
	Nov 17th	4 am	Situation normal -	
		12 noon	Casualties 2nd Colds Gds. A.D.C.R.S. Follett R.V.O & Major G.G. Davis Stewart M.C. wounded at duty	
			" " O.R. 1 Killed 2 wounded -	
			3rd Colds Gds. O.R. 2 " 1 missing	
			1st Irish Gds. O.R. 3 " 4 "	
			1 " 2 "	

WAR DIARY or INTELLIGENCE SUMMARY

Army Form C. 2118.

(Erase heading not required.)

Place	Date	Hour	Summary of Events and Information	Remarks and references to Appendices
	March 18	8 p.m.	Bde Divl Order No received ordering the Bde to capture ORION & FINCH trenches two small trenches — consisting chiefly of connected shell hole — in the front of the Coldstream sector — Verbal information of this enterprise had been received before — it was decided to detail the 2 Coldstream Gds to carry out the attack on 15/17th with a silent attack & to relieve the 8th Div on our right on 17/18, our Bn being fixed for another 24 hours — Bde was formed in the trenches another 24 hours —	254
		9 p.m.	Bde Order No 15 issued	254/a.

WAR DIARY or INTELLIGENCE SUMMARY

Army Form C. 2118.

(Erase heading not required.)

Instructions regarding War Diaries and Intelligence Summaries are contained in F.S. Regs., Part II. and the Staff Manual respectively. Title Pages will be prepared in manuscript.

Place	Date	Hour	Summary of Events and Information	Remarks and references to Appendices
S.23.b.4.9.	Nov 17th	4 pm	Quieter day than usual. The last two nights had been very cold with a hard frost & the ground had become dry. All trenches had been much improved & work was proceeding apace. As much material as possible was carried up to the front line but there was still a crying lack of trench boards.	
	Nov 18.	4 am	Situation normal.	
			During the morning a thaw set in & the country soon turned from good to very slippery going & later in the day into a sea of mud again. For this reason it was decided to cancel the operation planned for the capture of ORION & FINCH trenches.	
			Casualties: 2nd Lieut. J.D. WITON wounded. 2/Lieut. [---] o.R. wounded 1. 2/Coldm [---] o.R. " 5.	appx. 258
		2 pm	Bde Div Order 95 received.	
		4 pm	The usual amount of shelling during the day.	
		8 pm	During the night 18/19 the 1st Coldstream relieved 2nd Coldstream. The relief was not complete until 5.15 a.m. owing to the darkness of the night & the deep mud.	259

WAR DIARY or INTELLIGENCE SUMMARY

Army Form C. 2118.

Place	Date	Hour	Summary of Events and Information	Remarks and references to Appendices
S.23.b.4.9.	Nov 18th	12 mn	At 12 m.n. the left front coy of 2nd Wiltshires SPRING FAMILY was attacked by strong German patrols from FINCH trench. For two hours they tried to come on but were unable to do so & finally gave up the attempt. That was fortunate as rifles & Lewis guns had become clogged with mud.	
	Nov 19th	4am	Situation normal. The rain during the night had made things worse than ever. The ble came into the line. As it was almost impossible to get men or stores up to the front line it was decided to put every available man to trench board onto the continuation of the abode towards the right – as possible up to the front line.	
		12 noon	Casualties 2nd Gren Gds O.R. 3. Killed – 1st Cold Gds O.R. 2. " 3 wounded 2nd S.G. O.R. " 4 " 1 Missing 2nd I.G. O.R. 1 "	
		4 pm	A somewhat quieter day. 2nd Irish Gds relieved 2nd Gren Gds –	

Army Form C. 2118.

WAR DIARY
or
INTELLIGENCE SUMMARY
(Erase heading not required.)

Place	Date	Hour	Summary of Events and Information	Remarks and references to Appendices
J.23.c.4.9.	Nov 20th	4 am	Situation normal	
		12 noon	Casualties	
			Killed Wounded	
			2nd Pion. Bn. O.R. 1	
			1st Coy. Bn. 2 3	
			2nd P. Coy. 3"	
			2nd Tunl. Bn. 1	
			3	
		4 pm	Enemy artillery very active all day owing to the amount of movement going on everywhere. Weather dry & progress with work possible.	
	Nov 21st	4 am	Situation normal	
		12 noon	Casualties 1st Coy. Bn. O.R. K. nil Wded 1) Missing 4	
			2nd Tunl. Bn. O.R. K. 3 " 9 " 0	
		4 pm	A fairly quiet day owing to thick mist. During the night the 2nd Tunl. & 1st Coy. Bn. were relieved by 33rd & 31st Australians. There was the usual amount of shelling. However the relief which was not complete until 11.30 pm	

Army Form C. 2118.

WAR DIARY
or
INTELLIGENCE SUMMARY

(Erase heading not required.)

Place	Date	Hour	Summary of Events and Information	Remarks and references to Appendices
S.23.b.4.9 to (SAND)PITS Camp E.24.d	Nov 22nd	10 a.m.	Owing to the state of the ground there were many men who were unable to get back to their camps until late on the 22nd. The Sand Pits near WATERLOT Farm proved of the greatest value during this tour of the trenches. The men invariably prefer them to say — a copy of notes handed to incoming Bde is attached. Bde H.Q. closed at WATERLOT Farm & moved to the Sandpits —	APO 260
	Nov 23rd	2.15	Bde Resting — Conference at 3rd Bde Bde H.Q. MEAULTE for Brigadiers —	
	Nov 24th	11.30am	Conference for C.O.'s at Bde H.Q. Staff Capt. Capt. F.H. WITTS 1st R? Irish Gds joined as attached Staff Capt.	
	Nov 25th		Weather very wet & camp in a very bad state — as photographs to follow —	

2449 Wt. W14957/M90 750,000 1/16 J.B.C. & A. Forms/C.2118/12.

WAR DIARY
or
INTELLIGENCE SUMMARY

(Erase heading not required.)

Army Form C. 2118.

Place	Date	Hour	Summary of Events and Information	Remarks and references to Appendices
	Mar 25th	10 a.m.	Bde Div order 96 received	APR 25/1
	Mar 26th	8.30 p.m.	1st Bde Rds order No 72 issued	262
		4 p.m.	Sunday - service as usual - Bde Div. order No 97 received -	263
	Nov 27		3rd Coldstream Gds & 1st Irish Gds. moved to hutted camp at FORÊT) TRÉZ (L.2. a. & b.) These huts had been erected by & were taken over from the French - Men were more comfortable in these camps than for many months past - Lt. sin R.' O'Brien appointed Staff Captain - 1st and Gds Bde	
	Nov 28th			
	Nov 29th	6 p.m.	Bde Div Order No 98 received - Class I march tables issued to units ?	264

WAR DIARY
or
INTELLIGENCE SUMMARY

Army Form C. 2118.

Place	Date	Hour	Summary of Events and Information	Remarks and references to Appendices
	Nov 9th	10.30am	Brigadier inspected camps of 3rd Coldstream & 1st Irish Gds.	
		2.35pm	Provisional conference. The Major General pointed out the features of importance of SAILLY SAILLISEL - the necessity for distributing another gun in depth & protecting the right flank of the Division on	

J. V. Sereren
Brig General
Comdg 1st Guards Bde

DIVISIONAL OPERATION ORDERS

SECRET

"Q".
C.R.E.
1st Guards Brigade.
3rd Guards Brigade.
Pioneer Battalion.
A.D.M.S.
A.P.M.
Divnl. Train.
S.S.O.
O.C., Supply Column.

(244)

G.D. No. 2345/G.

(1). In continuation of G.301, one battalion 1st Guards Brigade and one battalion 3rd Guards Brigade will move by bus on the 6th November to XIV Corps area.

Destination and time of start for busses will be notified later.

Transport will move to-morrow to LONGPRE (just N.W. of AMIENS) where it will billet for the night 5th/6th.

On 6th it will move to DAOURS and billet there night of 6th/7th, moving on 7th to XIV Corps area.

Billeting at LONGPRE and DAOURS will be arranged by D.A.A.& Q.M.G. Times of march and route, each day, as convenient.

(2). Pioneer Battalion (4th Bn. Coldstream Guards) will return to the Division.

Personnel will arrive in XV Corps area by train on 6th November and will move to ST. MAULVIS.

Transport will march from ARGOEUVES to ST. MAULVIS on 7th November.

ACKNOWLEDGE.

C.P. Heywood.

4th November 1916.

Lieut. Colonel,
General Staff, Guards Division.

C.R.E.
1st Guards Bde.
2nd Guards Bde.
3rd Guards Bde.
Pioneer Bn.
"Q".
A.D.M.S.
A.D.V.S.
Signals.
Divnl. Train.
Supply Column.
A.P.M.
Camp Commandant.
Senior Supply Officer.
D.A.D.O.S.
Sanitary Section.

SECRET.

245

G.D. No.2440/G.

WARNING ORDER.

1. The Division will move up into XIV Corps Area, and will take over a portion of the line probably about November 12th.

2. (a) Transport of 2 Brigade Groups will move from present area on the 8th; Transport of 1 Brigade Group on 9th.

   (b) Personnel of 2 Brigade Groups will move by bus on 10th; Personnel of 1 Brigade Group on 11th.

   (c) Composition of Groups will be notified later.

3. C.R.E. Guards Brigades, Pioneer Battalion, A.D.M.S. and Camp Commandant will wire numbers of personnel (showing Officers and O.R.) to be moved by bus. Statement to reach Divisional Hd.Qrs. by 2 p.m. November 7th.

ACKNOWLEDGE.

6th November 1916.

Lieut-Colonel,
General Staff. Guards Divn.

SECRET.  Copy No. 3

GUARDS DIVISION ORDER NO. 88.

Reference Map 1/100,000 Sheets DIEPPE & AMIENS.

1. The transport and mounted portions of 1st and 3rd Guards Brigade Groups will move by road tomorrow to SAISSEVAL and AILLY SUR SOMME in accordance with March Table attached.

2. The transport of 76th Field Company R.E. will march with 3rd Guards Brigade Group.

3. The transport and mounted portions of 2nd Guards Brigade Group will move by road on the 9th instant to AILLY SUR SOMME in accordance with March Table attached.

4. The transport of 4th Bn. Coldstream Guards will march with Divisional Headquarters Group.

5. Baggage and supply sections of the train accompany their respective Brigade Groups.

ACKNOWLEDGE.

E Seymour Capt
Lieut-Colonel,
General Staff. Guards Divn.

7th November 1916.

Issued to Divnl. Signals at 4/10 p.m.

Copy No. 1 General Staff.
2 "Q".
3 1st Guards Brigade.
4 2nd Guards Brigade.
5 3rd Guards Brigade.
6 C.R.E.
7 Pioneer Battalion.
8 Divnl. Signals.
9 A.D.M.S.
10 A.D.V.S.
11. A.P.M.
12 Camp Commandant.
13 Divnl. Train.
14 Senior Supply Officer.
15 O.C. Supply Column.
16 Sanitary Section.
17 D.A.D.O.S.
18 XIV Corps.
19 Fourth Army.
20 XV Corps.
21 War Diary.

MARCH TABLE

FOR MOVEMENT OF TRANSPORT AND MOUNTED UNITS, ISSUED WITH GUARDS DIVISION ORDER NO. 88.

Date.	Formation.	Present Position.	Starting Point.	Time.	Route.	Destination.
8th.Novr. (A).	1st Guards Bde. Group. Transport, 1st Gds.Bde.	DROMESNIL area	HALLIVILLERS.	10 am.	HALLIVILLERS. CAMPS-en-AMIENOIS. HOLLIENS-VIDAME. BRIQUEMESNIL.	SAISSEVAL.
	4th Field Amb. less dismounted personnel.	VILLERS CAMPSART.				
8th.Novr. (B).	3rd Guards Bde. Group. Transport, 3rd Guards.Bde.	AVESNE area.	METIGNY.	10 am.	AIRAINES. SOUES. PICQUIGNY. AILLY-sur-SOMME.	AILLY-sur-SOMME.
	76th Field Coy.RE. (less dismounted personnel)	LALEU.				
	3rd Field Amb. (less dismounted personnel).	VERGIES.				
9th.Novr. (C).	2nd Guards Bde. Group. Transport, 2nd Gds.Bde.	TAILLY area.	L'ARBRE A MOUCHE.	10 am.	L'ARBRE A MOUCHE. LEQUESNOY. SOUES. PICQUIGNY. AILLY-sur-SOMME.	AILLY-sur-SOMME.
	Mobile Vet. Section.	TAILLY.				
	9th Field Amb. (less dismounted personnel).	L'ARBRE A MOUCHE.				

Page.2.

Date.	Formation.	Present Position.	Starting Point.	Time.	Route.	Destination.
9th.Novr.	(D). Divisional Hd.Qrs. Group.					
	Divnl. Hd. Qrs. (less dismounted personnel)	BELLOY ST. LEONARD.	East end of BELLOY village on BELLOY-WARLUS road.	10 am.	BELLOY ST.LEONARD. WARLUS. CAMPS-en-AMIENOIS. MOLLIENS VIDAME. BRIQUEMESNIL.	SAISSEVAL.
	Transport, Pioneer Battalion.	ST.MAULVIS.	—do—	10.10 am.	—do—	—do—

Date.	Formation.	Position.	Starting Point.	Time.	Route.	Destination.
9th.Novr.	(A)	SAISSEVAL.		12.30 pm.	AMIENS. VECQUEMONT. (FERRIERES SAVEUSE road available).	To XIV Corps Area.
9th.Novr.	(B).	AILLY-sur-SOMME.		12.30 pm.	AMIENS. VECQUEMONT.	—do—
10th.Novr.	(C)	AILLY-sur-SOMME.		8.30 am.	AMIENS. VECQUEMONT.	—do—
10th.Novr.	(D).	SAISSEVAL.		8.30 am.	AMIENS. VECQUEMONT. (FERRIERES-SAVEUSE road available).	—do—

SECRET.

AMENDMENT TO GUARDS DIVISION ORDER No. 88.

(1). The March Table issued with above order is cancelled and the attached substituted.

(2). Delete the words "to SAISSEVAL" in para. 1, which village is not now available for billets.

ACKNOWLEDGE.

                                            E Seymour Capt.
                                     for. Lieut.Colonel,

7th Novr. 1916.   General Staff, Guards Division.

Issued at 9 p.m. to

General Staff.	Divnl. Train.
"Q".	Senior Supply Officer.
1st Guards Brigade.	O.C., Supply Column.
2nd Guards Brigade.	Sanitary Section.
3rd Guards Brigade.	D.A.D.O.S.
C.R.E.	XIV Corps.
Pioneer Battalion.	Fourth Army.
Divnl. Signals.	XV Corps.
A.D.M.S.	War Diary.
A.D.V.S.	
A.P.M.	
Camp Commandant.	

AMENDED MARCH TABLE

FOR MOVEMENT OF TRANSPORT AND MOUNTED units, ISSUED WITH GUARDS DIVISION ORDER NO. 88.

Date.	Formation.	Present Position.	Starting Point.	Time.	Route.	Destination.
8th.Novr.	(A). 1st Guards Bde. Group. Transport, 1st Guards.Bde.	DROMESNIL area.	HALLIVILLERS.	10 am.	HALLIVILLERS. CAMPS-en-AMIENOIS. MOLLIENS-VIDAME. FOURDRINOY.	AILLY-sur-SOMME.
	4th Field Amb.less dismounted personnel.	VILLERS CAMPSART.				
	(B). 3rd Guards Bde. Group. Transport, 3rd Guards.Bde.	AVESNE area.	METIGNY.	10 am.	AIRAINES. SOUES. PICQUIGNY.	AILLY-sur-SOMME.
	76th Field Coy R.E. (less dismounted personnel)	LALEU.				
	3rd Field Amb. (less dismounted personnel)	VERGIES.				
9th.Novr.	(C). 2nd Guards Bde. Group. Transport, 2nd Guards.Bde.	TAILLY area.	L'ARBRE A MOUCHE.	10 am.	L'ARBRE À MOUCHE. LEQUESNOY. SOUES. PICQUIGNY. AILLY-sur-SOMME.	AILLY-sur-SOMME.
	Mobile Vet.Section.	TAILLY.				
	9th Field Amb. (less dismounted personnel).	L'ARBRE A MOUCHE.				

Page. 2.

Date.	Formation.	Present Position.	Starting Point.	Time.	Route.	Destination.
9th.Novr.	(D). Divnl. Hd.Qrs. Group.					
	Divnl.Hd.Qrs.(less dismounted personnel)	BELLOY ST.LEONARD.	East end of BELLOY village on BELLOY-VARLUS road.	10 am.	BELLOZ ST.LEONARD. L'ARBRE A MOUCHE. LEQUESNOY. SOUES. PICQUIGNY.	AILLY-sur-SOMME.
	Transport, Pioneer Battalion.	ST. MAULVIS.	—do—	10.10 am.	—do—	—do—
	(A).	AILLY-sur-SOMME.	To be fixed by officer Commanding Brigade Group concerned in the neighbourhood of billeting area.	12.30 pm.	AMIENS. VECQUEMONT.	DAOURS.
	(B).	AILLY-sur-SOMME.		12.50 pm.	AMIENS. VECQUEMONT.	—do—
10th.Novr.	(C).	AILLY-sur-SOMME.		8.30 am.	AMIENS. VECQUEMONT.	DAOURS.
	(D).	AILLY-sur-SOMME.		8.50 am.	AMIENS. VECQUEMONT.	—do—
	(A).	DAOURS.		10 am.	MERICOURT. VILLE.	CITADEL. SANDPITS.
	(B).	—do—		10.20 am.	MEAULTE. CARCAILLOT FARM.	
11th.Novr.	(C).	DAOURS.		9.30 am.	MERICOURT. VILLE.	MEAULTE.
	(D).	—do—		9.50 am.	MERICOURT.	TREUX. (Pioneers to SANDPITS).

SECRET. 248   Copy No 4

GUARDS DIVISION ORDER NO. 89.

1. The personnel of the Division will move by bus into XIV Corps area on 10th and 11th instant, in accordance with table attached.

2. The personnel of 1st and 3rd Guards Brigade Groups will embus on 10th instant, the personnel of 2nd Guards Brigade Group and Divisional Headquarters Group, on the 11th instant.

3. The composition of Brigade and Headquarter Groups is shewn in attached table.

4. Group Commanders will report completion of movement to Divisional Headquarters.

5. On completion of movements, units and formations will be disposed as follows:-

Divisional Headquarters   TREUX.

1st Guards Brigade Group   CITADEL.
   (less 2nd Bn. Coldstream Guards & 75th Field Coy.R.E.)

2nd Guards Brigade Group   MEAULTE.

3rd Guards Brigade Group   SANDPITS.
   (less 1st Bn. Welsh Guards & 55th Field Coy.R.E.)

6. Divisional Headquarters will close at BELLOY ST. LEONARD at 3 p.m. on the 10th instant, and re-open at the same hour at TREUX.

7. Debussing for all Groups will be carried out between MERICOURT and TREUX.

ACKNOWLEDGE.

CP Heywood
Lieut-Colonel,
9th November 1916.   General Staff. Guards Divn.

Issued at 2 a.m. to Divnl. Signals.

P.T.O

TIMETABLE OF BUSSES

FORMATION	PRESENT POSITION	ROUTE	DESTINATION	TIMETABLE OF BUSSES
(A) PERSONNEL of, 1st Guards Bde.) Machine Gun Coy.) T.M. Battery.) 4th Field Amb.)	DROMESNIL Area. VILLERS CAMPSART.	AMIENS, QUERRIEU, D.20.b.6.2, RIBEMONT, BUIRE, VILLE, (Busses to return via MERICOURT CORBIE VECQUEMONT.	Troops debus as in para. 7 and march to CITADEL via MEAULTE and CARCAILLOT FARM.	8.30 a.m. Busses for 1st Bn. I.G., M.G. Coy. and T.M.B. on CAMPS-EN-AMIENOIS - HORNOY road - Tail of column at HORNOY 9.15 a.m. Busses for remainder of (A) Group personnel on HORNOY - AUMONT road Tail at South end of AUMONT.
(B) PERSONNEL of, 3rd Guards Bde.) Machine Gun Coy.) T.M. Battery.) 75th Field Coy. R.E. 3rd Field Amb.	AVESNE Area. LALEU FRESNOY.	-do-	Troops debus as in para. 7 and march to SANDPITS via MEAULTE and CARCAILLOT FARM.	9.30 a.m. Busses for 1st Bn. G.G. on AIRAINES - OISEMONT road - Tail of column at WOIREL. 10 a.m. Busses for remainder of (B) Group personnel on EPAUMESNIL - ST.MAULVIS road - Tail of column at ST.MAULVIS.
(D) PERSONNEL of, Divnl. Hd.Qrs. Sanitary Section Salvage Section.	BELLOY ST.LEONARD.	-do-	Troops debus at TREUX.	9 a.m. Busses for (D) Group personnel at BELLOY ST.LEONARD CHURCH.
(C) PERSONNEL of, 2nd Guards Bde.) Machine Gun Coy.) T.M. Battery.) 9th Field Amb.	TAILLY Area. L'ARBRE A MOUCHE.	-do-	Troops debus as in para. 7 and march to MEAULTE.	8.30 a.m. Busses for 1st Bn. S.G. & 2nd Bn. I.G. on AIRAINES - CAMPS EN AMIENOIS road - Tail of column where WARLUS - MONTAGNE road cuts above road. 9.30 a.m. Busses for remainder of (C) Group personnel on AIRAINES - CAMPS EN AMIENOIS road: head at road junction to LALEU, facing South.

SECRET.   Copy No. 4

GUARDS DIVISION ORDER NO. 90.

1. Para. 4 Guards Division Order No. 88 is cancelled.

2. (a) The personnel 4th Bn. Coldstream Guards (Pioneers) will move into XIV Corps forward Area (SANDPITS) on 13th instant. The move will be either by rail or by bus.

   (b) The transport of this unit will move by road as follows:-

DATE	FROM	TO	ROUTE	REMARKS
11th.	ST.MAULVIS	AILLY SUR SOMME		(i) Route on 11th under orders of Officer Commanding.
12th.	AILLY SUR SOMME	DAOURS	AMIENS VECQUEMONT	
13th.	DAOURS	SANDPITS	MEAULTE CARCAILLOT FARM.	(ii) Billets in AILLY SUR SOMME will be arranged for by 20th Division.

ACKNOWLEDGE.

LMG

9th November 1916.

Issued to Signals at 1 p.m.

E Seymour Capt.
for Lieut-Colonel,
General Staff. Guards Divn.

Copy No. 1 General Staff.
   2 "Q".
   3 C.R.E.
   4 1st Guards Brigade.
   5 2nd Guards Brigade.
   6 3rd Guards Brigade.
   7 Pioneer Battalion.
   8 Divnl. Signals.
   9 A.D.M.S.
   10 A.D.V.S.
   11 A.P.M.
   12 Divnl. Train.
   13 Senior Supply Officer.
   14 O.C. Supply Column.
   15 Sanitary Section.
   16 D.A.D.O.S.
   17 XIV Corps.
   18 Fourth Army.
   19 XV Corps.
   20 War Diary.
   21 20th Division.
   22 Camp Commdt.

SECRET. (250)   Copy No .. 5.

GUARDS DIVISION ORDER NO. 91.

1. Guards Division (less Artillery) will relieve 17th Division (less Artillery) in the line on nights of 12th/13th and 13th/14th November.

2. 1st Guards Brigade will be on the right and will relieve 50th Inf. Bde. and ⅓ 51st Inf. Bde. 3rd Guards Brigade will be on the left and will relieve 52nd Inf. Bde. and ½ 51st Inf. Bde. 2nd Guards Brigade will be in reserve.

3. Reliefs will be carried out as shown in attached appendix. A table of routes and hours of starting will be issued later.

4. Divisional and inter Brigade Tactical Boundaries are shown on map issued to Guards Brigadiers, C.R.E., A.D.M.S., Pioneer Bn. and Divnl. Signals herewith.

    Boundaries in back areas will be notified later to all concerned.

5. Divisional and Guards Brigade Headquarters will be situated as follows:-

    Divisional Hd. Qrs.   BERNAFAY WOOD.
    Right Brigade Hd. Qrs.   S.18.d.5.2, present 50th and 51st
                                         Inf. Bde. Hd. Qrs.
    Left Brigade Hd. Qrs.   S.12.b.5.5, present 52nd Inf. Bde.
                                         Hd. Qrs.
    Reserve Brigade Hd. Qrs. MANSELL CAMP.

6. Relief of Field Coys. R.E. and Pioneer Bn. will be arranged between C.R.Es. Guards Division and 17th Division.

    Relief of Field Ambulances between A.Ds.M.S. Guards and 17th Divisions.

    Arrangements made to be notified to this office.

7. The Divisional front will be covered by 2 Artillery Groups, supporting right and left sectors respectively. Position of Artillery Group Hd. Qrs. will be notified later.

8. On and after November 16th, 2 Battalions 2nd Guards Brigade will be attached for tactical purposes to 1st Guards Brigade, and 2 Battalions 2nd Guards Brigade to 3rd Guards Brigade.

    The working of this Group system will form the subject of a separate order.

2.

9. On and subsequent to November 16th, G.Os.C. sectors will order moves of Battalions as required. It is not desirable that more than 1 Battalion from the front system of each sector should be relieved on any one night.

Camps available on and subsequent to 16th November are allotted as under:-

Right Sector.
(Camp A   1 Battalion.
(Camp H   2 Battalions.
(MANSELL CAMP   1 Battalion.

Left Sector.
(Camp D   1 Battalion.
(Camp F   1 Battalion.
(Camp H   1 Battalion.
(MANSELL CAMP   1 Battalion.

10. Defence Schemes and Secret Trench Maps will be taken over from Brigades in the line.

11. The date and hour at which Divisional Hd. Qrs. will close at TREUX and open at BERNAFAY WOOD will be notified later.

A C K N O W L E D G E .

Lieut-Colonel,
9th November 1916.   General Staff. Guards Divn.

Issued to Divnl. Signals at 6 p.m.

Copy No. 1 General Staff.   11 A.D.V.S.
        2 "Q".   12 Divnl. Train.
        3 G.D.A.   13 Senior Supply Officer.
        4 C.R.E.   14 A.P.M.
        5 1st Guards Brigade.   15 Sanitary Section.
        6 2nd Guards Brigade.   16 XIV Corps.
        7 3rd Guards Brigade.   17 8th Division.
        8 Pioneer Bn.   18 17th Division.
        9 Divnl. Signals.   19   Australian Divn.
       10 A.D.M.S.   20 War Diary.
                                    21 Camp Commandant.

APPENDIX TO ACCOMPANY GUARDS DIVISION ORDER NO. 91.

SHOWING POSITION OF UNITS, AND MOVEMENTS TAKING PLACE, ON EACH DAY.

	MEAULTE	SANDPITS	CITADEL	H Camp, (CAPNOY - MONTAUBAN Road).	CORPS CAMP, MONTAUBAN.	F CAMP, MONTAUBAN.	TRONES WOOD A CAMP	D CAMP	FRONT SYSTEM
11th.	Bde.H.Q. 2nd Gds.Bde. 2 Bns, 4 Bns, 2rd Gds.Bde.	Bde. H.Q. 3rd Gds.Bde. --- 1 Bn, 3rd Gds.Bde. to D CAMP.	Bde. H.Q. 1st Gds.Bde. 1 Bn 1st Gds Bde 1 Bn, 1st Gds.Bde. to A CAMP. 1 Bn, 1st Gds.Bde. to F CAMP.						
12th.	Bde.H.Q. 2nd Gds.Bde. 3 Bns, 2nd Gds.Bde. --- 1 Bn, 2nd Gds.Bde. to CAMP H.	Bde.H.Q. 3rd Gds.Bde. 1 Bn, 3rd Gds.Bde. --- 1 Bn, 3rd Gds.Bde. to H CAMP.	Bde.H.Q. 1st Gds.Bde. --- 1 Bn, 1st Gds.Bde. to H CAMP.		1 Bn, 1st Gds.Bde. 1 Bn, 3rd Gds.Bde.	1 Bn, 1st Gds.Bde.	1 Bn, 1st Gds.Bde. into the line.	1 Bn, 3rd Gds.Bde. into the line.	
13th.	Bde.H.Q. 2nd Gds.Bde. 3 Bns, 2nd Gds.Bde.	Bde.H.Q. 3rd Gds.Bde. --- 3rd Gds.Bde. into line.	Bde.H.Q. 1st Gds.Bde. 1st Gds.Bde. into line.	1 Bn, 1st Gds.Bde. 1 Bn, 2nd Gds.Bde. --- 1 Bn, 3rd Gds.Bde. into line.	1 Bn, 1st Gds.Bde. 1 Bn, 3rd Gds.Bde.	1 Bn, 1st Gds.Bde. into line.			1 Bn, 1st Gds.Bde. 1 Bn, 3rd Gds.Bde.

2.

DATE	MEAULTE	SANDPITS	CITADEL	H CAMP (CARNOY-MONTAUBAN road)	CORPS CAMP MONTAUBAN	F CAMP MONTAUBAN	TRONES WOOD A CAMP	TRONES WOOD D CAMP	FRONT SYSTEM
14th.	Bdo. H.Q. 2nd Gds.Bde. 3 Bns, 2nd Gds.Bde.	1 Bn, 3rd Gds.Bde.		1 Bn, 1st Gds.Bde. 1 Bn, 2nd Gds.Bde.	1 Bn, 1st Gds.Bde. 1 Bn, 3rd Gds.Bde.				2 Bns, 1st Gds.Bde. 2 Bns, 3rd Gds.Bde.
15th.	Bdo.H.Q. 2nd Gds.Bde. to MANSELL CAMP. 1 Bn, 2nd Gds.Bde. to H CAMP. 2 Bns, 2nd Gds.Bde. to MANSELL CAMP.	1 Bn, 3rd Gds.Bde. to F CAMP.		1 Bn, 2nd Gds.Bde. 1st Gds.Bde. 1 Bn, 1st Gds.Bde. 3rd Gds.Bde. to A CAMP.	1 Bn, 1st Gds.Bde. into line. 1 Bn, 3rd Gds.Bde. into line.				1 Bn, 1st Gds.Bde. 1 Bn, 3rd Gds.Bde. 1 Bn, 1st Gds.Bde to H CAMP 1 Bn, 3rd Gds.Bde to D CAMP

SECRET.   Copy No ..5..

GUARDS DIVISION ORDER NO. 92.

1. Routes and times of starting in connection with moves ordered in Guards Division Order No. 91 are shown on table attached. Where possible units will take cross country tracks.

2. Units of Guards Division will come under command of 17th Division on arrival in Camps "A", "D", "F" and "H".

3. Hd.Qrs. 2nd Guards Brigade will move from MEAULTE to MANSELL Camp on November 14th and not as ordered in Guards Division Order No. 91.

   They will be clear of MEAULTE by 12 noon.

4. Map references of Camps:-

Camp "A"	S.23.d.6.8.
Camp "B"	S.23.d.5.3.
Camp "D"	S.23.c.8.5.
Camp "F"	S.28.c.4.4.
Camp "H"	A.8.a.8.2.
MANSELL Camp	F.11.b.

5. Right Group Artillery supporting Divisional front is located at T.25.a.8.5.

   Left Group at T.25.a.7.6.

6. G.O.C. Guards Division will take over command of the line at 10 a.m. on November 14th, at which hour Divisional Hd.Qrs. will close at TREUX and open at BERNAFAY WOOD.

ACKNOWLEDGE.

                                                    C.P.Heyward.
                                                    Lieut-Colonel,
11th November 1916.   General Staff. Guards Divn.

Issued to Divnl. Signals at 2/20 a.m.

Copy No.			
1	General Staff.	12	A.P.M.
2	"Q".	13	Camp Commandant.
3	G.D.A.	14	Divnl. Train.
4	C.R.E.	15	Senior Supply Officer.
5	1st Guards Brigade.	16	C.C. Supply Column.
6	2nd Guards Brigade.	17	Sanitary Section.
7	3rd Guards Brigade.	18	D.A.D.O.S.
8	Pioneer Battalion.	19	17th Division.
9	Divnl. Signals.	20	XIV Corps.
10	A.D.M.S.	21	War Diary.
11	A.D.V.S.	22	1st Australian Divn.

DATE	UNIT	FROM	TO	ROUTE	REMARKS
A) 11th.	1 Bn. 3rd Guards Bde.	SANDPITS.	"D" Camp.	FRICOURT Cemetery cross roads at F.9.a.5.5, Road junction at F.4.c.5.4, MAMETZ, MONTAUBAN.	Bn. to arrive at "D" Camp at 4 p.m. Already notified to 3rd Guards Bde.
	1 Bn. 2nd Guards Bde.	CITADEL,	"A" Camp.	-do-	Bn. to arrive at "A" Camp at 3.30 p." Already notified to 1st Guards Bde.
(B)	1 Bn. 1st Guards Bde.	-do-	"F" Camp.	-do-	The Bn. to be clear of FRICOURT Cemetery cross roads (F.9.a.. at 11 a.m. Already notified to 1st Guards Bde.

2

DATE	UNIT	FROM	TO	ROUTE	REMARKS
(D) 12th.	1 Bn. 2nd Guards Bde.	MEAULTE.	"H" Camp.	Troops will march by main ALBERT - MARICOURT road, and CARNOY. Transport by road junction F.4.c.5.4 - MAMETZ, road junction S.27.c.6.3 (COSY CORNER).	Starting point LE CARCAILLOT cross roads at E.18.a at 1 p.m. To take over Camp now occupied by 10th Bn. West Yorks. Troops must march from F.18.c.6.2 to "A" Camp in file - 200 yards interval between Coys.
(E)	1 Bn. 3rd Guards Bde.	SANDPITS.	"H" Camp.	-do-	Starting point LE CARCAILLOT cross roads at E.18.a at 1.30 p.m. To take over Camp now occupied by 9th Bn. Northumberland Fusiliers. Troops must march from F.18.c.6.2 in file - 200 yds. interval between Coys.
(F)	1 Bn. 1st Guards Bde.	CITADEL.	"H" Camp.	-do-	Starting point cross roads F.9.a 3 p.m. Bn. to follow in rear of (E). To take over Camp now occupied by 7th Bn. Border Regt. Troops to march from F.18.c.6.2 in file, 200 yds. between Coys.
(G) (H)	1 Bn.1st Gds.Bde. 1 Bn.3rd Gds.Bde.	"A" Camp. "D" Camp.	Line. Line.		Under Brigade arrangements. -do-
(I)	76th Field Coy. R.E.	SANDPITS.	LONGUEVAL.	FRICOURT Cemetery, road junction F.4.c.5.4, MAMETZ - MONTAUBAN - GUILLEMONT.	To start at 9 a.m. Transport by CARNOY, road junction F.18.c.6.2 cross roads at A.22.a.8.3, BERNAFAY CORNER, GUILLEMONT.
(J)	55th Field Coy. R.E.	"H" Camp.	-do-	-do-	To start at 10 a.m. Transport as above, Troops must move in file from "H" Camp as far as MONTAUBA
(K)	75th Field Coy. R.E.	"H" Camp.	-do-	-do-	To start at 10.25 a.m. Troops mu move in file from "H" Camp as fa MONTAUBAN. Transport as above.

DATE	UNIT	FROM	TO	ROUTE	REMARKS.
13th.	(L) Bde. H.Q. 3rd Guards Bde.	SANDPITS.	Line.		Under Brigade arrangements. To relieve 52nd Inf.Bde. Hd.Qrs.
	(M) Bde. H.Q. 1st Guards Bde.	CITADEL.	Line.		Under Brigade arrangements. To relieve 50th Inf.Bde. Hd.Qrs.
	(N) 1 Bn. 3rd Guards Bde.	"H" Camp.	Line.	MONTAUBAN – BERNAFAY CORNER.	Bn. to start at 10 a.m. It is suggested that dinner should be at BERNAFAY WOOD. Troops move thence under Brigade arrangements into the line.
	(O) 1 Bn. 1st Guards Bde.	"F" Camp.	Line.		Under Brigade arrangements.
14th.	(P) Bde. H.Q. 2nd Guards Bde.	MEAULTE.	MANSELL Camp.		Under Brigade arrangements. To be completed by noon.
	(Q) 1 Bn. (1st Welsh Gds.) 3rd Gds.Bde.	MANSELL Camp.	"F" Camp.	MAMETZ – MONTAUBAN.	Bn. will arrive at "F" Camp. at 5 p.m.

4.

DATE	UNIT	FROM	TO	ROUTE	REMARKS
15th (R).	Pioneer Bn. 3 Coys.	SANDPITS.	WATERLOT FARM	Details later.	Pioneers, 17th Div. vacate forward Camps on 14th. Arrangements for taking over will be made between C.R.Es. concerned direct.
(S)	1 Coy.	SANDPITS.	"F" Camp.		
(T)	1 Bn. 2nd Guards Bde.	MEAULTE.	"H" Camp.	FRICOURT Cemetery, cross roads at F.9.a.5.5, Road junction at F.18.c.6.2, CARNOY.	Starting point 9.15 a.m. LE CARCAILLOT cross roads at E.18.a. Transport marches by road junction F.4.c.5.4, MAMETZ, road junction at S.27.c.7.3.
(U)	1 Bn. 2nd Gds. Bde.	MEAULTE.	MANSELL Camp.	FRICOURT Cemetery cross roads at F.9.a.5.5.	Starting point LE CARCAILLOT cross roads 1 p.m.
(V)	1 Bn. 2nd Gds. Bde.	MEAULTE.	MANSELL Camp.	-do-	Starting point LE CARCAILLOT cross roads 1.30 p.m.
(W)	1 Bn. 3rd Gds. Bde.	SANDPITS.	"D" Camp.	MAMETZ, MONTAUBAN.	Starting point LE CARCAILLOT cross roads at E.18.a. at 9 a.m.
(X)	1 Bn. 1st Gds. Bde.	"H" Camp.	"A" Camp.		Bn. to start at 8.30 a.m.
(Y)	1 Bn. 1st Gds. Bde.	Corps Camp.	Line.		Brigade arrangements.
(Z)	1 Bn. 3rd Gds. Bde.	"F" Camp.	Line.		-do-

<u>Note</u>. Under existing conditions it has been found that troops do not average more than two miles an hour in marching to the forward Camps.

SECRET.   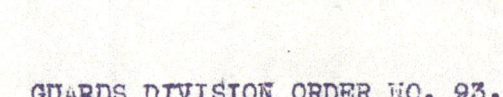   Copy No. 4

GUARDS DIVISION ORDER NO. 93.

1.   1st Guards Brigade will on the night of November 18th/19th capture ORION TRENCH and FINCH TRENCH.

Should conditions for the attack be unfavourable on the night of 18th/19th, G.O.C. 1st Guards Brigade is at liberty to postpone the operation.

2.   Detailed arrangements as to cooperation of machine guns and extension of front of 1st Guards Brigade to the South, will be made between 1st Guards Brigade and Left Brigade of Right Division, XIV Corps.

3.   Artillery support for the operation will be arranged between 1st Guards Brigade and Right Group, Left Artillery XIV Corps.

4.   Prisoners will be handed over to Corps Cage at A.8.a.6.8.

5.   Hour of zero will be notified later.

ACKNOWLEDGE.

                                    C P Heywood
                                    Lieut-Colonel,
15th November 1916.   General Staff. Guards Divn.

Issued to Signals at 6.39 p.m.

Copy No. 1   General Staff.   9   "Q".
         2   Left Artillery, XIV Corps. 10   Signals.
         3   C.R.E.   11   A.P.M.
         4   1st Guards Brigade.   12   8th Division.
         5   2nd Guards Brigade.   13   29th Division.
         6   3rd Guards Brigade.   14   4th Australian Divn.
         7   Pioneer Bn.   15   XIV Corps.
         8   A.D.M.S.   16   War Diary.

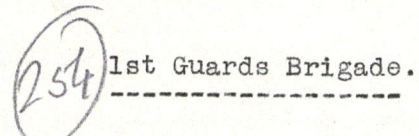

G.D. No.2473/G.

1st Guards Brigade.
----

1. The extent and object of the operation to be carried out by 1st Guards Brigade, outlined by the Major-General yesterday, will be as under:-

   A. The object of the operation is to capture ORION TRENCH and FINCH TRENCH and join these trenches up with our present front line at about N.35.A.1.1 on the right and to SPRING TRENCH on the left. By the capture of the above two trenches observation will be gained on to the LE TRANSLOY Line.

   B. XIV Corps have sanctioned your taking over such portions of 8th Division front as you may require for the operation.

   C. 8th Division will co-operate by joining up AUTUMN TRENCH with the new line in the neighbourhood of N.35.A.2.2.

   D. Fourth Army Intelligence Summary of November 12th, states that 28th Ersatz Regiment, opposite the portion of our line in question, will be relieved on night of 16th/17th November. It is for consideration whether this night would not be a favourable one for the operation.

2. The Major-General will come to your Headquarters about 3 p.m. tomorrow to discuss details of the operation.

   Points on which he would like to receive information are:-

   A. Date proposed for the operation.

   B. Extent of front to be taken over from 8th Division and when to be taken over.

   C. Point of junction with 8th Division in new line, i.e. the point to which 8th Division are to dig a new trench from AUTUMN TRENCH.

D. Artillery preparation and support required.

[signature]

Lieut-Colonel,

13th November 1916.   General Staff. Guards Divn.

Aeroplane photographs taken on 10/11/16 are enclosed.

SECRET.  Copy No. 5.

WARNING ORDER.

GUARDS DIVISION ORDER NO. 94.

1. The Division will be relieved by the 5th Australian Division, relief to be completed by night of 20th/21st November.

   (a) Relief of front line Battalions of Left Brigade sector will be carried out on night of 19th/20th, relief of front line Battalions of Right Brigade sector on night of 20th/21st.

   (b) On completion of relief the Division will be disposed in the area "H" Camp - CITADEL - SANDPITS - MEAULTE.

2. About December 1st, the Division will take over the SAILLY - SALLISEL Sector from the French.

A C K N O W L E D G E.

C.P.Heyward.

Lieut-Colonel,
16th November 1916.   General Staff. Guards Divn.

Issued to Signals at 1.15 p.m.

Copy No. 1 General Staff.
       2 "Q".   9 Divnl. Signals.
       3 Left Artillery, XIV Corps. 10 A.D.M.S.
       4 C.R.E.   11 A.D.V.S.
       5 1st Guards Brigade.   12 Divnl. Train.
       6 2nd Guards Brigade   13 S.S.O.
       7 3rd Guards Brigade.   14 Sanitary Section.
       8 Pioneer Bn.   15 War Diary.

SECRET.

AMENDMENT TO GUARDS DIVISION ORDER NO. 94.

Relief of the Division will be completed by night of 21st/22nd November.

Relief of front line Battalions, Left Brigade sector will be carried out on night of 20th/21st, relief of front line Battalions, Right sector on night of 21st/22nd.

ACKNOWLEDGE.

CP Heywood.
Lieut-Colonel,
General Staff, Guards Divn.

16th November 1916.

Issued to   General Staff.
"Q".   Divnl. Signals.
Left Artillery, XIV Corps   A.D.M.S.
C.R.E.   A.D.V.S.
1st Guards Brigade.   Divnl Train.
2nd Guards Brigade.   S.S.O.
3rd Guards Brigade.   Sanitary Section.
Pioneer Bn.   War Diary.

SECRET.

SECRET.

Copy No. 5

GUARDS DIVISION ORDER NO. 95.

1. The Division (less Artillery) will be relieved by the 5th Australian Division (less Artillery) relief to be completed on the night of 21st/22nd November.

   (A) 2 Front Line Battalions of 3rd Guards Brigade (Left) Sector will be relieved on night of 20th/21st November by 2 Battalions 15th Australian Infantry Brigade.

   (B) 2 Front Line Battalions of 1st Guards Brigade (Right) Sector will be relieved on night of 21st/22nd November by 2 Battalions, 8th Australian Infantry Brigade.
   Details of reliefs to be arranged between Brigades.

2. Movements of Guards Brigades into back area will be carried out as shown in Appendix "A" attached.

3. Distribution on completion of relief is shown in Appendix "B". Movements of 5th Australian Division in Appendix "C".
Table of routes and hours of starting will be issued later.

4. (A) CITADEL and SANDPITS are available for details on and after November 19th.

   (B) No accommodation at MEAULTE will be available before November 21st.

   (C) MANSEL CAMP will be cleared of all Units and details Guards Division by 12 Noon on 21st, with exception of Units engaged in Hutting.

   (D) "F" Camp after vacation by 1st Bn:Grenadier Guards on 21st will remain under charge of the Division. "Q" will detail necessary party for its custody.

   (E) "C" Camp will be clear of all Units and details Guards Division by 12 Noon on 22nd.

5. C.R.E. will arrange details of relief of R.E., with C.R.E., 5th Australian Division.

    A.D.M.S., will arrange details of relief of medical units with A.D.M.S., 5th Australian Division.

    Arrangements made to be notified to this office.

6. Defence Schemes, Secret Maps and Air Photographs will be handed over to relieving Brigades. - Those of 2nd Guards Brigade will be sent to Divisional Head Quarters by 5 p.m. on November 21st.

7. All Trench Stores will be handed over on relief, receipts taken, and lists sent to Divisional Head Quarters.

/8.

8.   All orders, for movements of Battalions in Right and Left Brigade Groups into back area, will be issued by G.O.C. Right and Left Brigade Groups respectively.

9.   G.O.C. Guards Division will hand over command of the line to G.O.C. 5th Australian Division at 10 a.m., on November 22nd at which hour Divisional Head Quarters will close at BERNAFAY WOOD and open at TREUX.

A C K N O W L E D G E.

                                                                        [signature]

H.Q. Guards Division.
18th November, 1916.   Lieut-Colonel,
                                        General Staff, Guards Division.

Issued to Signals at .... p.m.

Copy No. 1 General Staff.
       2 "Q".
       3 Left Artillery, XIV Corps.
       4 C.R.E.
       5 1st Guards Brigade.
       6 2nd Guards Brigade.
       7 3rd Guards Brigade.
       8 O.C. Pioneer Battalion.
       9 O.C. Divnl: Signals.
      10 A.D.M.S.
      11 A.D.V.S.
      12 A.P.M.
      13 O.C. Divnl: Train.
      14 O.C. Supply Column.
      15 Senior Supply Officer.
      16 Camp Commandant.
      17 Sanitary Section.
      18 D.A.D.O.S.
      19 XIV Corps.
      20 29th Division.
      21 5th Australian Division.
      22 War Diary.

Guards Camp Commandants
      23   MANSEL CAMP
      24   H Camp
      25   F Camp

APPENDIX 'A'.

MOVEMENTS OF GUARDS BRIGADES DURING RELIEF.

DATE	IN THE LINE	A & B CAMPS	D CAMP	F CAMP	H CAMP	MANSEL CAMP	CITADEL	SANDPITS	MEAULTE
19th.	2/Gren.Gds. to H Camp.	2/Irish Gds. to Line.	2 Coys. 1/Scots Gds. to Line. 1/Scots Gds. (less 2 Coys.) to H Camp.		3/Gren.Gds. to SANDPITS. 4/Gren.Gds. to SANDPITS.				
	2 Coys. 1/Welsh Gds. to H Camp.				3/Welsh Gds. to Sandpits				
20th	2 Coys. 1/Scots Gds. 1/Welsh Gds. (less 2Coys) to H Camp. 1/Gren.Gds. to F Camp. 3rd Bde.H.G. Coy.and 3rd Bde.T.M.Bty. to F Camp.			2/Scots Gds. to SANDPITS.	1/Irish Gds. to SANDPITS.				
21st.	3rd Gds.Bde. Hd.Qrs. to MEAULTE. 2/Irish Gds. 1/Coldstream Gds. to H Camp.			1/Gren.Gds. to MEAULTE. 3rd Gds.Bde. H.G.Coy. & T.M.Bty. to MEAULTE.	2/Gren.Gds. to MEAULTE. 1/Welsh Gds. to MEAULTE.	2/Cold:Gds. to MEAULTE. 3/Gren.Gds. to CITADEL.	2nd Gds.Bde. Hd.Qrs. to CITADEL. 2nd Gds.Bde. H.G.Coy. & T.M.Bty. to CITADEL.		
22nd.	1st Gds.Bde. Hd.Qrs. to SANDPITS.			1st Gds.Bde. H.G.Coy. & T.M.Bty. to SANDPITS.					

APPENDIX "B".

DISTRIBUTION ON COMPLETION OF RELIEF.

"H". CAMP	CITADEL.	SANDPITS.	MEAULTE.
1st Bn: Coldstream Guards. 1st Bn: Scots Guards. 2nd Bn: Irish Guards.	2nd Guards Bde.Hd.Qrs. " " M.G.Coy. " " T.M.Bty. 3rd Bn: Grenadier Guards. 4th Bn: Coldstream Guards. (PIONEERS). 1 Field Company, R.E. 1 -do- Ambulance.	1st Guards Bde.Hd.Qrs. " " M.G.Coy. " " T.M.Bty. 3rd Bn: Coldstream Guards. 1st Bn: Irish Guards. 4th Bn: Grenadier Guards. 2nd Bn: Scots Guards. 1 Field Company, R.E. 1 -do- Ambulance.	3rd Guards Bde.Hd.Qrs. " " M.G.Coy. " " T.M.Bty. 2nd Bn: Grenadier Guards. 2nd Bn: Coldstream Guards. 1st Bn: Grenadier Guards. 1st Bn: Welsh Guards. 1 Field Company, R.E. 1 -do- Ambulance.

Divisional Head Quarters
TREUX.

NOTE.- Accommodation for 3 Field Companies and Pioneer Battalion as shown above is available, but it will depend on requirements of labour for hutting what proportion of R.E. remains in forward area.

APPENDIX "C".

MOVEMENTS OF 5TH AUSTRALIAN DIVISION
as far as it affects
GUARDS DIVISION.

DATE. November.	MOVEMENT.
19th.	2 Battalions, 15th Australian Infantry Brigade from back area to "A", "B" and "D" Camps (in afternoon).
20th.	2 Battalions, 15th Australian Infantry Brigade from "A", "B" and "D" Camps to Line - (Left Sector).
	2 Battalions, 8th Australian Infantry Brigade from back area to "A", "B" and "D" Camps (in afternoon).
21st.	2 Battalions, 8th Australian Infantry Brigade from "A", "B" and "D" Camps to line - (Right Sector).
	1 Battalion, 15th Australian Infantry Brigade ⎫ from back area to Camps "A", "B" and "D"
	1 Battalion, 8th Australian Infantry Brigade ⎭ (in afternoon).

SECRET.   261   Copy No. 5

WARNING ORDER.

GUARDS DIVISION ORDER NO. 96.

1. The Division (less Artillery) will relieve portions of the 152nd French Division in the line, relief to be completed by morning of December 4th.

2. (a) The frontage to be taken over by the Division is from U.8.A.8.3 to T.6.B.7.2.

   This front is at present held by 3 Battalions, with 3 Battalions in support in the area MORVAL - COMBLES - LEUZE WOOD - FALFEMONT FARM.

   (b) The 20th French Corps holds the line South of U.8.A.8.3.

   The 29th Division will be holding as far East as T.6.B.7.2 by the morning of December 2nd.

3. The Group System as laid down in G.D. No.2450/G, para. 1 will continue in force. Tours of duty of Brigade Headquarters and Machine Gun Coys. are shewn in attached appendix.

   G.Os.C. Groups will issue all orders for movements of Battalions of their Groups from their present positions and also warning and other orders in connection with the relief.

4. The relief will be carried out as under:-

   (a) Left Group (3rd Guards Brigade) will take over the frontage U.1.D.8.3 - T.6.B.7.2 with 2 Battalions, relieving 1 Battalion 296th Regiment and 1 Battalion 125th Regiment in front line.

   (b) Right Group (2nd Guards Brigade) will take over the front U.8.A.8.3 - U.1.D.8.3 with 1 Battalion, relieving 1 Battalion 114th Regiment in front line.

/(c).

(c) One Battalion, Right Group, will move into support in COMBLES Area, and one Battalion Left Group into support in area BOULEAUX WOOD - LEUZE WOOD - FALFEMONT FARM.

Details of accommodation available will be communicated later.

(d) Movements in connection with relief will be as under:-

Dec. 1st.

2 Battalions Left Group from present area to Camps at MALTZHORN FARM (A.6.A and B).

Dec. 2nd.

2 Battalions Left Group from MALTZHORN FARM into line.

1 Battalion Right Group and 1 Battalion Left Group from present area to MALTZHORN FARM.

Dec. 3rd.

1 Battalion Right Group from MALTSHORN FARM into line.

1 Battalion Left Group MALTZHORN FARM to area BOULEAUX WOOD - FALFEMONT FARM.

1 Battalion Right Group from back area to COMBLES Area.

5. The movements and distribution of the remaining 7 Battalions of the Division are not yet settled but will probably be as follows:-

1 Battn. Right Group)
1 Battn. Left Group) to MALTZHORN FARM on Dec. 3rd.

2 Battns. Right Group)
2 Battns. Left Group) to BRONFAY FARM on Dec. 3rd.
                         (F.29.A.)

1 Battalion Right Group to remain in present area pending the taking over of another Battalion front to the South shortly after the 4th December.

/6.

6. G.Os.C. Groups will forward a statement to this office showing which Battalions of their Groups they wish to carry out the various reliefs mentioned in para. 4.

7. (a) Divisional and inter-Brigade Boundaries of forward area are shown on attached map. Boundaries of rear area will be notified later.

(b) Headquarters will be located as under:-

Divisional Hd.Qrs.   ARROW HEAD COPSE, S.30.B.2.2.

Right Guards Brigade) COMBLES CATACOMBS.
Group Hd. Qrs.   )

Left Guards Brigade) BOIS DORE, T.20.D.4.2.
Group Hd. Qrs.   )

The position of Reserve Guards Bde. Hd. Qrs. is not yet fixed.

8. C.R.E. will arrange with C.R.E. 152nd French Division details of relief of R.E. and Pioneer Battalion.

A.D.M.S. will arrange with A.D.M.S. 152nd French Division (HARDECOURT) details of relief of medical units.

Arrangements to be submitted to this office.

A C K N O W L E D G E.

C.P. Heywood
Lieut-Colonel,
25th November 1916.   General Staff. Guards Divn.

Issued to Signals at 6.30 p.m.

Copy No. 1 General Staff.   8. Pioneer Battalion.
         2 "Q".   9. A.D.M.S.
         3 G.D.A.   10. Signals.
         4 C.R.E.   11. XIV Corps.
         5 1st Guards Brigade. 12. 152nd Divn. (French).
         6 2nd Guards Brigade. 13. 9th Corps. (French).
         7 3rd Guards Brigade. 14. War Diary.

****

"C" Form (Duplicate).
MESSAGES AND SIGNALS.

Army Form C. 2123.
(In books of 50's in duplicate.)
No. of Message..................

Service Instructions.

Charges to Pay. £ s. d.

Office Stamp.

Handed in at............................Office............m. Received............m.

TO 101 Gaurds Bde

Sender's Number	Day of Month	In reply to Number	A A A

FROM
PLACE & TIME   2nd Gd Bde

"C" Form (Duplicate).
MESSAGES AND SIGNALS.
Army Form C. 2123.
(In books of 50's in duplicate.)
No. of Message..................

Service Instructions.

Handed in at................ Office........ m. Received........ m.

TO M Gots Bde

Sender's Number	Day of Month	In reply to Number	A A A
Ref	Gots	Div	warning order
No 9/7	aaa	for	night of
7/8	read	night of	6/7
aaa	ack		

FROM
PLACE & TIME   Gots div
              11.50

SECRET.	Copy No. 5.

WARNING ORDER.

GUARDS DIVISION ORDER NO: 97.

Right Guards Brigade Group will on the night of 6/7th/8th December extend their right as far as U.14.B.9.6. relieving portion of the 20th French Corps.

Details of boundaries, etc., will be notified later.

P. Heyworth
Lieut-Colonel,
General Staff, Guards Division.

26th November, 1916.

Issued to Signals at 2.40 p.m.

Copy No. 1 General Staff.
2 "Q".
3 G.D.A.
4 C.R.E.
5 1st Guards Brigade.
6 2nd Guards Brigade.
7 3rd Guards Brigade.
8 O.C. Pioneer Battalion.
9 A.D.M.S.
10 Divnl: Signals.
11 War Diary.

264/A

SECRET.   Copy No ..5..

GUARDS DIVISION ORDER NO. 100.

1. On the night of December 7th/8th the following adjustments of front will be carried out.

(a) Right Guards Brigade Group will extend its left as far as U.8.A.3.8. The Boundary between Guards Brigade Groups will then run as shown on map attached to G.D. No.2570/G.

(b) Adjustment of Machine Gun Companies will be made so that they support their respective Brigade Group frontage.

2. Details of above reliefs to be arranged between Brigades concerned.

ACKNOWLEDGE

C.P. Heywood
Lieut-Colonel,
5th December 1916.   General Staff. Guards Divn.

Issued to Signals at 8 p.m.

Copy No. 1   General Staff.
        2   "Q".
        3   G.D.A.
        4   C.R.E.
        5   1st Guards Brigade.
        6   2nd Guards Brigade.
        7   3rd Guards Brigade.
        8   Pioneer Battalion.
        9   A.D.M.S.
       10   War Diary.

SECRET.   G.D. No.2561/G.

"Q".   A.P.M.
G.D.A.   Divnl. Train.
C.R.E.   Senior Supply Officer.
1st Guards Brigade.   O.C. Supply Column.
2nd Guards Brigade.   D.A.D.O.S.
3rd Guards Brigade.   XIV Corps.
Pioneer Battalion.   29th Division.
Divnl. Signals.   9th French Corps.
A.D.M.S.   152nd French Divn.
A.D.V.S.   War Diary.

---

1. Table showing times of starting and routes in connection with moves ordered in Guards Division Order No. 98 is attached.

2. (a) No troops will move East of a line GUILLEMONT - HARDECOURT before 4 p.m.

    (b) Troops moving on roads East of MEAULTE will march in file with intervals of 200 yards between Companies and 500 yards between Battalions.

ACKNOWLEDGE.

E. Seymour.
Captain,
30th November 1916.   General Staff, Guards Divn.

DATE	UNIT.	FROM.	TO.	ROUTE.	REMARKS.
Dec.1st.	3rd Gren.Gds.	FORKED TREE.	MALTZHORN FARM.	BRAY - MARICOURT.)	Brigade arrangements. Leading troops not to enter MARICOURT before 11 a.m. Head of transport will pass CARCAILLOT FARM at 10.30 a.m. and march via MAMETZ and MONTAUBAN to A.2.a.
	2nd Scots Gds.	-do-	-do-	-do-	
	3rd Gren.Gds.) 2nd Scots Gds.)	MALTZHORN.	LINE.		Troops to be clear of MALTZHORN by 4 p.m.
	3rd Cold.Gds.	FORKED TREE.	MALTZHORN FARM.	BRAY - MARICOURT.	To start at 12 noon. Takes over Camp vacated by 3rd Gren Gds Transport starts at same time and marches via CARCAILLOT FARM - MAMETZ & MONTAUBAN to A.2.a
Dec.2nd.	1st Scots Gds.	CARNOY WEST CAMPS.	MALTZHORN FARM.	BERNAFAY CORNER.	To start at 2.30 p.m. Camp to be clear by 3 p.m. Takes over Camp vacated by 2nd Scots Gds.
	2nd Gren.Gds.	MEAULTE.	CAMP 108, BRONFAY.	BRAY.	To start at 9 a.m. Head of transport to pass CARCAILLOT FARM at 11 a.m. and march via MAMETZ - MONTAUBAN to A.2.a.
	1st Welsh Gds.	MEAULTE.	CAMP 108, BRONFAY.	BRAY.	To start at 10 a.m. Head of transport to pass CARCAILLOT FARM at 11.15 a.m. and march via MAMETZ MONTAUBAN to A.2.a.

DATE.	UNIT.	FROM.	TO.	ROUTE.	REMARKS.
Dec.3rd.	3rd Cold.Gds.	MALTZHORN.	LINE.		To be clear of MALTZHORN Camp by 4 p.m.
	1st Scots Gds.	—do—	BOULEAUX WOOD.		To be clear of MALTZHORN Camp by 4 p.m.
	1st Irish Gds.	FORKED TREE.	MALTZHORN.	BRAY - MARICOURT.	To start at 11.45 a.m. Takes over Camp vacated by 3rd Cold.Gds. Head of transport will pass CARCAILLOT FARM at 1 p.m. and march via MAMETZ - MONTAUBAN to A.2.a.
	4th Gren.Gds.	SANDPITS.	MALTZHORN.	LE CARCAILLOT - FRICOURT CEMETERY - MARICOURT.	To start at 12 noon. Takes over Camp vacated by 1st Scots Gds. Transport marches via MAMETZ - MONTAUBAN to A.2.a.
	1st Guards Bde. Headquarters, Machine Gun Coy. Trench Mortar Bty.	—do—	MANSEL CAMP.		Brigade arrangements.
	2nd Cold.Gds.	MEAULTE.	COMBLES.	LE CARCAILLOT - MARICOURT - BERNAFAY CORNER - GUILLEMONT.	To start at 9 a.m. To halt in BERNAFAY Area under Brigade arrangements. Transport to pass CARCAILLOT FARM at 10 a.m. and march via MAMETZ - MONTAUBAN to A.2.a.
	Pioneer Bn.	CITADEL.	WEDGE WOOD, (COMBLES).	BRAY - MARICOURT.	To start at 8.30 a.m. To halt in BERNAFAY Area.

SECRET.   Copy No ..5..

GUARDS DIVISION ORDER NO. 99.

1. (a)   Left Guards Brigade Group will on the night of 5th/6th December extend its right as far as U.8.A.8.3, relieving all troops of Right Guards Brigade Group in front line.

   (b)   On completion of the above relief, Right Group will maintain one Company at BOIS DE LA HAIE, and one Company about T.28.B.3.3 (COMBLES). Left Group will maintain one Company at BOIS DE LA HAIE.

   (c)   Accommodation for 2 Battalions Right Group at MALTZHORN FARM will be available on night of 5th/6th December.

   This will not interfere with normal accommodation available for Left Group.

2. (a)   On night of 6th/7th December, Right Guards Brigade Group will relieve with 2 Battalions those portions of the French 39th Division between U.14.B.9.6 and U.8.A.8.3. This front is at present held by 2 Battalions in front line and one in Support.

   Details of relief to be arranged between G.O.C. 2nd Guards Brigade and G.O.C. 78th French Inf. Bde. (Hd.Qrs. MOUCHOIR COPSE, T.24.B.5.9).

   (b)   Arrangements for Artillery support will be notified later.

   (c)   C.R.E. will get into touch with C.R.E. 39th French Division as regards R.E. arrangements; similarly A.D.M.S. will get in touch with A.D.M.S. 39th French Division as regards medical arrangements.

   (d)   Map shewing inter-Brigade and Southern Divisional Boundary on completion of relief on night of 6th/7th December will be issued shortly.

P.T.O.

2.

ACKNOWLEDGE.

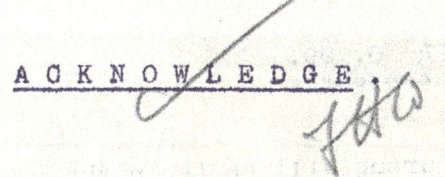
C F Heyward
Lieut-Colonel,
General Staff. Guards Divn.

29th November 1916.

Issued to Signals at 8 p.m.

Copy No.			
1	General Staff.	9	A.D.M.S.
2	"Q".	10	Signals.
3	G.D.A.	11	XIV Corps.
4	C.R.E.	12	29th Division.
5	1st Guards Brigade.	13	XX French Corps.
6	2nd Guards Brigade.	14	39th French Divn.
7	3rd Guards Brigade.	15	War Diary.
8	Pioneer Battalion.		

****

"C" Form (Duplicate). Army Form C. 2123.
(In books of 50's in duplicate.)

MESSAGES AND SIGNALS. No. of Message ....

Charges to Pay. £ s. d.

Office Stamp.

Service Instructions.

Handed in at .... Office .... m. Received .... m.

TO

Sender's Number	Day of Month	In reply to Number	AAA

[illegible]

97 aaa Appendices A and B

1st Gds Bde Group M G

Coy and T M Battery will

move on December 3rd

to Transit Camp

F H B and not as stated

I.H.W.

[illegible]

FROM

PLACE & TIME

Wt. 432—M437 500,000 Pads. H W V 5/16 Forms/C.2123.

SECRET.   Copy No. 5

(264)

GUARDS DIVISION ORDER NO. 98.

1.   The Division (less Artillery) will relieve portions of the 152nd French Division in the line, relief to be completed by 6 a.m. on December 4th, in accordance with paras: 2, 3, 4 and 7 of Guards Division Order No. 96.

2.   Movements of Guards Brigades in connection with the relief are shown in Appendix attached.

A table giving routes and hours of starting will be issued later.

3.   Units of Guards Division will come under command of 152nd French Division on arrival at or East of MALTZHORN FARM (A.6.A & B).

4.   Camps are allotted to Guards Brigade Groups as follows on and after December 3rd:-

Right Group.	MALTZHORN FARM	-	1 Battalion.
	CARNOY WEST	-	2 Battalions.
	CAMP 108 (BRONFAY FARM)		1 Battalion.
Left Group.	MALTZHORN FARM	-	1 Battalion.
	CAMP 108 (BRONFAY FARM)		1 Battalion.
	MEAULTE	-	1 Battalion.

After 6 p.m. on December 6th, accommodation for 1 Battalion only of Right Group will be available at CARNOY WEST.

5. Accommodation for Support Battalions of Right and Left Groups in the COMBLES - LEUZE WOOD Area is allotted as follows:-

Support Battalion. Right Group.

1 Company.   COMBLES TRENCH (T.27.B).
2 Companies. LEUZE WOOD.
1 Company.   MALTZHORN FARM.
Battn.Hd.Qrs.T.27.B.6.0.

Support Battalion. Left Group.

3 Companies. BOULEAUX WOOD.
1 Company.   T.26.B.2.8.
Battn.Hd.Qrs.T.21.C.9.5.

The French Battalions in occupation of the above accommodation will be moving back on the early morning of December 3rd.

Advanced parties of Supporting Battalions Right and Left Groups will be at 152nd Division Hd.Qrs. T.20.D.3.2 at 9 a.m. on December 3rd, where guides will be provided by 152nd Division to point out accommodation available.

6. (a)   The Divnl. front will be supported by French Artillery up to night of 6th/7th December on which night relief of French Field Artillery by British Artillery will be completed.

   (b)   Arrangements have been made for French Artillery Liaison Officers to remain at Brigade and Battalion Headquarters.

7. 2 Battns. ~~~~~~~~ at Camp 108 (BRONFAY)
   1 Battn. ~~~~~~~~ at MEAULTE
   1st Guards Brigade M.G. Company.
   1st Guards Brigade T.M. Battery.

   will form Divnl. reserve under command of G.O.C. 1st Guards Brigade.

Cancelled
G.D.
2576/g.
2/12/16

8. A General Staff Officer, Guards Division will be at Headquarters, 152nd French Division from 3 p.m. December 2nd, until completion of relief on morning of December 4th.

9. G.Os.C. Right and Left Guards Brigade Groups will take over command of their sectors at 9 a.m. on December 4th.

G.O.C. Guards Division will take over command of the line at 9 a.m. on December 4th, at which hour Divisional Headquarters will close at TREUX and open at ARROWHEAD COPSE.

A C K N O W L E D G E.

CPHeywood
Lieut-Colonel,
General Staff, Guards Divn.

29th November 1916.

Issued to Signals at 4.30 p.m.

Copy No. 1 General Staff.
2 "Q".
3 G.D.A.
4 C.R.E.
5 1st Guards Brigade.
6 2nd Guards Brigade.
7 3rd Guards Brigade.
8 Pioneer Battalion.
9 Divnl. Signals.
10 A.D.M.S.
11 A.D.V.S.
12 A.P.M.
13 Divnl. Train.
14 Senior Supply Offr.
15 O.C. Supply Column.
16 D.A.D.O.S.
17 XIV Corps.
18 29th Division.
19 9th French Corps.
20 152nd French Divn.
21 War Diary.

****

Brigade
OPERATION ORDERS

243.

Copy No. 1

1st Guards Brigade Order No. 85.

Ref. Map - DIEPPE 1/100,000.   October 31st, 1916.

1. The Brigade will parade to-morrow, November 1st, for the Review of the Guards Division by H. R. H. the Duke of Connaught.

2. March Table is attached.

3. Dress -

    Officers - Sam Browne Belt (one cross sling) without revolvers; walking sticks or gloves except for mounted Officers. Dismounted Officers will not wear spurs.

    Other Ranks - Belt - side Arms - rolled waterproof sheets and rifles.

4. Sgt. Majors and one (right) marker for each half Company of Battalions and Machine Gun Company, and a right marker for Trench Mortar Battery will report to Brigade Major at DROMESNIL Windmill at 9-30 A.M.

    ACKNOWLEDGE.

                                                    Captain,
                                Brigade Major, 1st Guards Brigade.

Issued through Signals at :- 2.30 p.m.

Copy No. 1 2nd Bn. Grenadier Guards.
         2 2nd Bn. Coldstream Guards.
         3 3rd Bn. Coldstream Guards.
         4 1st Bn. Irish Guards.
         5 Bde., Machine Gun Company.
         6 1st Guards T. M. Battery.
         7 Staff Captain.
         8 Guards Division.
         9, 10, 11, 12 Retained.

1.

MARCH TABLE.

Order of March.	Route.	Starting point.	Time.	Remarks.
3/Coldstream Gds.	SELINCOURT - DROMESNIL Road.	Road junction 400 yds. N.W. of D of DROMESNIL.	10.15 a.m.	
2/Coldstream Gds.	direct.	"	10.18 a.m.	To keep clear of main street in DROMESNIL.
1/Irish Guards.	HORNOY - BOIS - RAULT - O of B. de la CORROYE.	"	10.13 a.m.	
2/Grenadier Gds.	AUMONT - SELINCOURT.	"	10.22 a.m.	Not to enter SELINCOURT until 3/Cold. Gds. are clear.
Bde. M.G.Coy. T.M.Battery.	As for 1/Irish Gds.	"	10.24 a.m.	Machine Gun Company will parade with Gun Limbers.

N.B. (a) Battalions will move on their markers from the right passing by the S.E. corner of the parade ground, and will form up on their markers facing right in Quarter Column of half Coy's.

(b) Brigade Machine Gun Coy. and T.M.Battery will halt on the S. side of the BELLOY - VILLERS Road opposite their markers - as soon as 2nd Guards Brigade have passed down this road they will move straight on their markers.

SECRET.   Copy No. 14

1st Guards Brigade Order No. 86.

7th November 1916.

Ref. Maps - DIEPPE & AMIENS
           Sheets 1/100,000.

1. The 1st Line Transport of Units will move in accordance with attached March Table to XIV Corps Area under the Bde., Transport Officer.

2. Baggage and supply sections of the Train will accompany Units.

3. Billeting arrangements are being made by "Q" Branch [Guards Divn] and a Staff Officer will meet the Transport on arrival at the destination each day.
Bde., Transport Officer will arrange to ride forward and meet this Officer.

4. (a) Personnel of the Brigade will move by bus on Nov: 10th. Details will be notified later.
   (b) Lorries have been ordered to take Lewis Gun carts and extra equipment on 10th inst., as follows :-
       Battalions   - 2 each -
       M.G.Company - 1 -
       T.M.Battery - 1.
   (c) Arrangements about blankets will be notified later.

ACKNOWLEDGE.

Captain,
Brigade Major, 1st Guards Brigade.

Issued through Signals at :- 7.30 pm

Copy No. 1 2nd Bn. Grenadier Gds.,
         2 2nd Bn. Coldstream Gds., (for information.)
         3 3rd Bn. Coldstream Gds.,
         4 1st Bn. Irish Guards.
         5 Bde., Machine Gun Coy.,
         6 1st Guards T.M.Batty.,
         7 No. 4 Field Ambulance.
         8 No. 3 Coy., Train.
         9 Guards Division.
        10 Bde., Transport Officer.
        11 Staff Captain.
        12 O.C., Signals.
        13 & 14 Retained.

1.

2nd Bn. Grenadier Guards.
1st Bn. Irish Guards.
Bde., Machine Gun Company.
No. 4 Field Ambulance.

    Reference March Table issued with Brigade Order No. 86, the following instructions have been sent direct to Bde., Transport Officer -

    Destination on Nov: 8th will be AILLY-sur-SOMME and not SAISSEVAL.

    On Nov: 10th the Transport will march to the CITADEL via MERICOURT L'ABBE and VILLE.

                                        Captain,

8th Nov: 1916.   Brigade Major, 1st Guards Brigade.

MARCH TABLE.

Date.	Order of March.	Starting Point.	Time.	Route.	Destination.	Remarks.
Nov:8th.	2/Gren.Gds. 3/Cold.Gds. 1/Irish Gds. Bde.M.G.Coy.	Cross roads N of HALLIVILLERS. " " "	10 A.M. " " "	(HALLIVILLERS -) (CAMPS-on-AMIENOIS) (MOLLIENS-VIDAME) (BRIQUEMESNIL.)	SAISSEVAL.	
	No.3 Coy.Train	"	10-10 A.M.	"	"	Not to enter HORNOY until M.G.Coy. are clear.
	No.4 Fld.Amb.,	"	"	"	"	Not to pass road junc. 1/2 mile N.W. of HORNOY on the
	Brigade H.Q.,	"	"	"	"	VILLERS rd. until No.3 Coy.Train are clear.
Nov:9th.	As ordered by Bde.Tpt.Officer.	As ordered by B.T.O.	12-30 P.M.	AMIENS - VECQUEMONT.	DAOURS.	
Nov.10th.	Orders for this move will be sent later to-night.					

SECRET.   Copy No. 12

1st Guards Brigade Order No. 87.

9th November 1916.

Ref. Maps - AMIENS & DIEPPE 1/100,000.
ALBERT Combined Sheet 1/40,000.

1. The personnel of the Brigade will move by bus into XIV Corps Area on 10th inst., in accordance with March Table attached.

2. The Brigade will debus between TREUX and MERICOURT and will then march to the CITADEL (F.21.b). Units will move off independently as soon as they have debussed.
Route - MEAULTE - CARCAILLOT Farm.

3. Billeting parties will travel on the leading bus allotted to each Unit and will be ordered to report to the Staff Captain at the CAMP COMMANDANTS Office at the CITADEL as soon as possible after debussing.

4. Completion of movements will be reported to this Office.

5. Brigade H.Q., will close at DROMESNIL at 7-30 A.M. and open at the CITADEL on completion of the journey.

ACKNOWLEDGE.

Captain,
Brigade Major, 1st Guards Brigade.

Issued at :- 2 pm.

Copy No. 1 2nd Bn. Grenadier Guards.   Copy No. 8 Guards Division.
        2 2nd Bn. Coldstream Guards.   9 Bde., Transport Officer.
        3 3rd Bn. Coldstream Guards.   10 Staff Captain.
        4 1st Bn. Irish Guards.   11 O.C., Signals.
        5 Bde., Machine Gun Company.   12, 13 & 14 Retained.
        6 1st Guards T. M. Battery.
        7 No. 4 Field Ambulance.

1.

MARCH TABLE.

Unit.	Embussing Place.	Route for Busses.	Remarks.
2/Gren.Gds.,	HORNOY - AUMONT Road just S. of AUMONT.	AMIENS - QUERRIEU - RIBEMONT - BUIRE - VILLE. (Busses to return by MERICOURT - CORBIE - VECQUEMONT.	To be formed up in column of route with head of Battn. facing S. at Southern end of AUMONT on HORNOY Road at 8-30 A.M.
3/Cold.Gds.	"	"	Head of Battn. to be at cross roads 1/2 mile South of L of SELINCOURT at 8-30 A.M.
1/Irish Gds.,	HORNOY - CAMPS Road just N. of H. of HORNOY.	"	To be formed up in column of route North of H of HORNOY and clear of HORNOY - CAMPS Road at 9 A.M.
M.G.Company.	"	"	To be formed up in rear of 1st Bn. Irish Guards.
T.M.Battery.			
No.4 Fld.Amb.,	As for 2/Gren.Gds.	"	To be at cross roads 1/2 mile South of L of SELINCOURT at 8-30 A.M. moving by most convenient route.
Brigade H.Q.,	"	"	To move to cross roads 1/2 mile South of L of SELINCOURT in rear of 3rd Bn. Coldstream Guards.

SECRET.   Copy No. 14

(251)

1st Guards Brigade Order No. 88.

November 9th, 1916.

Ref. Map - ALBERT 1/40,000.

1. The 1st Guards Brigade will relieve 50th Infantry Brigade and half the 51st Infantry Brigade on the nights of 12/13th and 13/14th of November.

2. A Table is attached showing movement of Battalions up to November 15th. Details of routes and times etc., will be forwarded later.

3. All Trench Stores, Secret Maps, Defence Schemes, etc., will be taken over.

4. On November 13th, Brigade H.Q., will move to S.18.d.5.2. present 50th and 51st Brigade H.Q.,

5. A Conference will be held at the earliest possible opportunity.

6. When the relief of 17th Division is complete the Camps at the disposal of the Right Group will be :-

    "A" Camp TRONES Wood   - 1 Battn.,
    "H" Camp MONTAUBAN - CARNOY Road   - 2 Battn's.,
    Mansell Camp near MINDEN POST   - 1 Battn.,

ACKNOWLEDGE.

Captain,

Brigade Major, 1st Guards Brigade.

Issued to Signals at :- 9 p.m.

Copy No. 1 2nd Bn. Grenadier Gds.,   Copy No. 9 Guards Division.
         2 2nd Bn. Coldstream Gds.,   10 3rd Guards Brigade.
         3 3rd Bn. Coldstream Gds.,   11 Camp Commandant.
         4 1st Bn. Irish Guards.   12 Staff Captain.
         5 Bde., Machine Gun Company.   13 O.C., Signals.
         6 1st Guards T. M. Battery.   14, 15 & 16 Retained.
         7 50th Infantry Brigade.
         8 51st Infantry Brigade.

MOVEMENT TABLE.

Date.	Unit.	From.	To	Remarks.
Nov: 11th.	3/Cold.Gds.,	CITADEL.	TRONES Wood "A" Camp.	
	1/Irish Gds., Bde.M.G.Coy. & T.M.Battery.	"	"F" Camp MONTAUBAN.	
Nov: 12th.	2/Gren.Gds.	"	"H" Camp at the Craters on MONTAUBAN - CARNOY Rd.	
	3/Cold.Gds.	TRONES Wood.	Left Sub-sector.	
	Half Bde.M.G.Coy.	"F" Camp MONTAUBAN.	Left Sub-sector.	
Nov: 13th.	Brigade H.Q.,	CITADEL.	Line - S.18.d.5.2.	
	1/Irish Gds.	"F" Camp.	Right Sub-Sector.	
	Half Bde.M.G.Coy.	"F" Camp.	Right Sub-Sector.	
Nov: 14th.	No Movement.			
Nov: 15th.	2/Cold.Gds.	Corps Camp MONTAUBAN.	Left Sub-sector.	
	3/Cold.Gds.	Left Sub-sector.	"H" Camp MONTAUBAN.	
	2/Gren.Gds.	"H" Camp MONTAUBAN.	TRONES Wood.	

SECRET.  Copy No. 14

Supplement to 1st Guards Brigade Order No. 88.

11th November 1916.

1. A more detailed Movement Table to the above Order is issued herewith and should be substituted for that previously issued.

2. On completion of relief of 7th East Yorks. the 3rd Bn. Coldstream Guards and part of M.G.Company will come under Orders of G.O.C., 50th Infantry Brigade until 10 A.M. on 13th inst.,

3. (a) The Brigade Transport Officer will meet the Brigade Transport Officer of 50th Infantry Brigade at 10 A.M. tomorrow.

   (b) He will ascertain when and by what Units the Lines will be vacated.

   (c) He will report to these H.Q., as soon as possible after he has been round the Lines.

   (d) The Transport Lines of the 50th Infantry Brigade are at A.2.b.6.2. and will be the permanent Lines for Units of this Brigade.

4. Work Platoons will be held ready to report for work under 75th Field Coy., R.E. as soon as required - Work Platoons of Battn's. in front line and "A" Camp only will be required for work.

5. Headquarters of Right Group supporting the Division Front are at T.25.a.8.5.

6. Brigade H.Q., will close at the CITADEL and open at S.18.d.5.2. just East of WATERLOT Farm at 9 A.M. on Nov: 13th.

ACKNOWLEDGE.

Captain,
Brigade Major, 1st Guards Brigade.

Issued at :- 8.30 p.m.

No. 1 2nd Grenadier Gds.,
    2 2nd Coldstream Gds.,
    3 3rd Coldstream Gds.,
    4 1st Irish Gds.,
    5 Bde., M.G.Company.
    6 1st Gds. T.M. Bty.,
    7 Guards Division.

No. 8 3rd Guards Brigade.
    9 50th Infantry Brigade.
   10 51st Infantry Brigade.
   11 Bde., Transport Officer.
   12 Staff Captain.
   13 O.C., Signals.
   14, 15 & 16 Retained.

1.

MOVEMENT TABLE.

Date.	Unit.	From.	To.	Route.	Remarks.
Nov:12th.	2/Gren.Gds.	CITADEL. A.8.a.8.2.	"H" Camp. A.8.8.2.	Troops to march by main ALBERT - MARICOURT Rd. and CARNOY - Transport by Rd.junc. F.4.c.5.4. - MAMETZ and Rd.junc.S.27.c.6.3.	(a) Head of Bn. to pass cross roads F.9.c.5.5. at 3 P.M. marching in rear of a Bettn. of 3rd Guards Bde. (b) After passing F.18.c.6.2. Troops to march in file with 200 yds. between Coy's. (c) Billeting party to be sent in advance to "H" Camp to take over from 7th Bn. Border Regt.and to arrange for billeting of T.M.Battery.
	1st Gds.T.M.Bty.	"	"	"	(a) An Officer to report to H.Q. 2nd GREN.Gds. at CITADEL at 9 A.M. for instructions as regards billeting. (b) To move in rear of 2nd Gren.Gds. - A lorry has been asked for.
	3/Cold.Gds.	"A" Camp.	Right Sub-Sector.	Direct.	(a) To take over from 7th Bn.East Yorks and right half of 7th Yorkshire Regt. from N.35.a.0.4. to N.34.a.2.0 N.28.d.5.5. Battn. H.Q. at N.34.c.2.0 (b) Details of relief to be arranged direct. (c) O.C. and Coy. Commdrs. to be at H.Q. 50th Inf.Bde. East of WATERLOT Fm. at 8 A.M. on 12th inst.
	1st Gds.Bde. M.G.Company.	"F" Camp.	"	"	(a) Arrangements direct with O.C. 50th M.G.Coy. (b) On completion of relief to have 4 guns in front line - 4 in ROSE Trench Line - 4 in NEEDLE Line.

Date	Unit.	From.	To.	Route.	Remarks.
Nov:13th.	Brigade H.Q.	CITADEL.	WATERLOT Fm.F.9.a.5.5.	-	To pass cross roads F.9.a.5.5. at 10 A.M.
	1/Irish Gds.	"F" Camp.	Left Sub-Sector.	Direct.	(a) To take over from right half of 7th Yorkshire Regt. and from 8th South Staffords from N.28.d.5.5. to N.28.b.1.7. Battn.H.Q. at junc. of WINDMILL Trench and NEEDLE Trench. (b) Details of relief to be arranged direct. (c) O.C. and Coy.Commdrs. to be at H.Q. 51st Inf.Bde. near WATERLOT Fm. at 8-30 A.M. on 13th inst.,
	Remainder of Bde.M.G.Coy.	"F" Camp.	Left Sub-Sector.	Direct.	(a) Arrangements direct. (b) On completion of relief to have 2 guns in GUSTY Trench - 1 in ROSE Line - 1 in NEEDLE Line.
Nov:14th.	No Movement.				
Nov:15th.	2/Gren.Gds.	"H" Camp.	"A" Camp, TRONES WOOD, MONTAUBAN.		(a) Battn. to march off at 8-30 A.M; from "H" Camp and to move by Coy's. at 200 yds. interval. (b) To send billeting party in advance.
"	2/Cold.Gds.	Corps Camp.	Right Sub-Sector.	Direct.	(a) All details to be arranged direct.- Time of movements to be notified to these H.Q.
"	3/Cold.Gds.	Right Sub-Sector.	"H" Camp.	Direct.	(a) Relief to be arranged direct. (b) To take over Camp vacated by 2/Gren.Gds.- Billeting party to take over at 8 A.M.

S E C R E T. 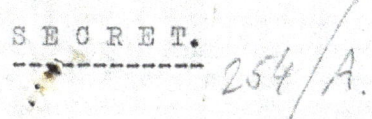   Copy No. 14

254/A.

1st Guards Brigade Order No. 89.

Ref. Map - 57 C. S.W. 1/20,000.   15th November 1916.

1. On the night of Nov: 18th/19th, 2nd Coldstream Guards will carry out a minor operation with the object of capturing ORION Trench and FINCH Trench.

2. Special Maps and Aeroplane Photographs are forwarded to the Battalion concerned.

3. Zero hour will be notified later to those concerned - It will probably be about 8 P.M. on 18th inst.,

4. (a) There will be no intense bombardment before Zero and only after Zero if called for.

   (b) From this date up to Zero, Right Group will keep up intermittent fire on the trenches concerned with a view to destroying as much as possible the enemy's works and morale without arousing his suspicions. Certain suspected Machine Gun positions communicated to Right Group will also be specially dealt with.

   (c) From Zero the suspected Machine Gun positions will be kept under continuous shrapnel fire.

   (d) If Infantry require a barrage after the assault has taken place they will send up a coloured Very Pistol Light, the colour of which will be made known later.

5. On the night of 17th/18th, 2nd Coldstream Guards will take over SUMMER Trench, at present held by 24th Brigade. Arrangements for the taking over of this trench will be made direct between O.C's. concerned.

Battalion H.Q., of the Left Battalion of 24th Brigade are at N.34.c.1.9.

MACHINE GUNS.

6. (a) O.C., 1st Guards Bde., Machine Gun Company will arrange to place two guns in SPRING Trench with a view to protecting the left flank of the attack and to bring fire to bear on the ground East of FINCH and ORION Trenches.

   (b) The 88th Machine Gun Company are arranging for a gun in AUTUMN Trench to protect the right flank of the attack and also to bring fire to bear on the ground East of FINCH and ORION Trenches.

CONSOLIDATION/

- 2 -

CONSOLIDATION.

7. (a) As soon as the position has been captured, covering parties with Lewis Guns should be pushed forward and the consolidation of the captured trenches begun.
A communication trench will be dug back from ORION to ZENITH Trench.

   (b) The 2nd Coldstream Guards will arrange to dig out from SPRING Trench to join up with the N. end of FINCH ST.,

   (c) The 24th Brigade will dig out from AUTUMN Trench and join up with the right of the attack on the SUNKEN Road about N.35.a.5.5.

RELIEF.

8. (a) The 1st Coldstream Guards will relieve the 2nd Coldstream Guards on the night of 18th/19th.

   (b) The relief of supporting Coys. will be carried out by 7-30 P.M. on 18th.

   (c) Coys. of 1st Coldstream Guards which are to relieve assaulting Coys. of 2nd Coldstream Guards will be accommodated in WINDMILL Trench West of NEEDLE - COW Trench - and the following trenches - PEN - MAIL - TIMES - PUNCH.
O.C., 2nd Coldstream Guards will have suitable portions of these trenches reconnoitred.

   (d) The relief of assaulting Coys. will be complete by 4 A.M.

   (e) SUMMER Trench will be re-occupied by 88th Brigade. Relief to be complete by 4 A.M.

MEDICAL ARRANGEMENTS.

9. An additional bearer party from Field Ambulance will be at Battalion H.Q., 2nd Coldstream Guards, at 7 P.M. on 18th inst.,

ACKNOWLEDGE.

Captain,
Brigade Major, 1st Guards Brigade.

Issued at :- 8.30 p.m.

Copy No.		Copy No.	
1	2nd Bn. Grenadier Guards.	8	Guards Division.
2	2nd Bn. Coldstream Guards.	9	3rd Guards Brigade.
3	3rd Bn. Coldstream Guards.	10	24th Infantry Brigade.
4	1st Bn. Irish Guards.	11	Right Group.
5	Bde. Machine Gun Company.	12	75th Field Coy., R.E.
6	1st Bn. Coldstream Guards.	13	Staff Captain.
7	2nd Bn. Irish Guards.	14, 15 & 16	Retained.

SECRET.

Supplement to 1st Guards Brigade Order No. 89.

Two sections 75th Field Coy., R.E. are at the disposal of O.C., 2nd Coldstream Guards for the wiring of ORION and FINCH Trenches after their capture.

O.C., 2nd Coldstream Guards will arrange to have two guides at H.Q., Left Battn., (2nd Gren.Gds.) at 6 P.M. tomorrow, 17th inst., to show R.E. to their assembly positions which will be allotted to them by O.C., 2nd Coldstream Guards. The R.E. will carry up their wiring material and reconnoitre the position tomorrow night. They will return to their assembly positions on the night of the attack before Zero under Orders to be issued by O.C., 2nd Coldstream Guards.

Issued to all recipients of Order No. 89.

Captain,

16th November 1916.

Brigade Major, 1st Guards Brigade.

SECRET.   Copy No. 14.

Supplement to 1st Guards Bde., Order No. 89.
17th Nov: 1916.

Ref. para. 3. Zero will be 8 P.M. on 18th inst.,

Ref. para. 4. (d). A Blue Rocket will be the Signal for the
               Artillery barrage to be put down.
               A Green Asteroid Rocket will be the Signal
               for the Artillery barrage to cease.

Add para. 4. (e). Right Group will detail a Liaison Officer to report at
                 H.Q. 2nd Coldstream Guards at 6 P.M. on 18th inst.,

Ref. para. 5. 2nd Coldstream Guards will not take over SUMMER Trench.

Para. 8. (e) is cancelled.

Substitute following for para. 9 :-
     No. 4 Bearer Post will take over all wounded from the Regimental
     Stretcher Bearers at NEEDLE Dump if required and on receipt of
     a priority message addressed - No. 4 Bearer Post Z.8.

Add para. 10. All details for co-operation between 2nd Coldstream Gds.,
              and O.C., Battn. on their right will be made direct
              between Officers Commanding Battalions concerned.
ACKNOWLEDGE.

                                                              Captain,
                                        Brigade Major, 1st Guards Brigade.

Issued to all recipients of Order No. 89.

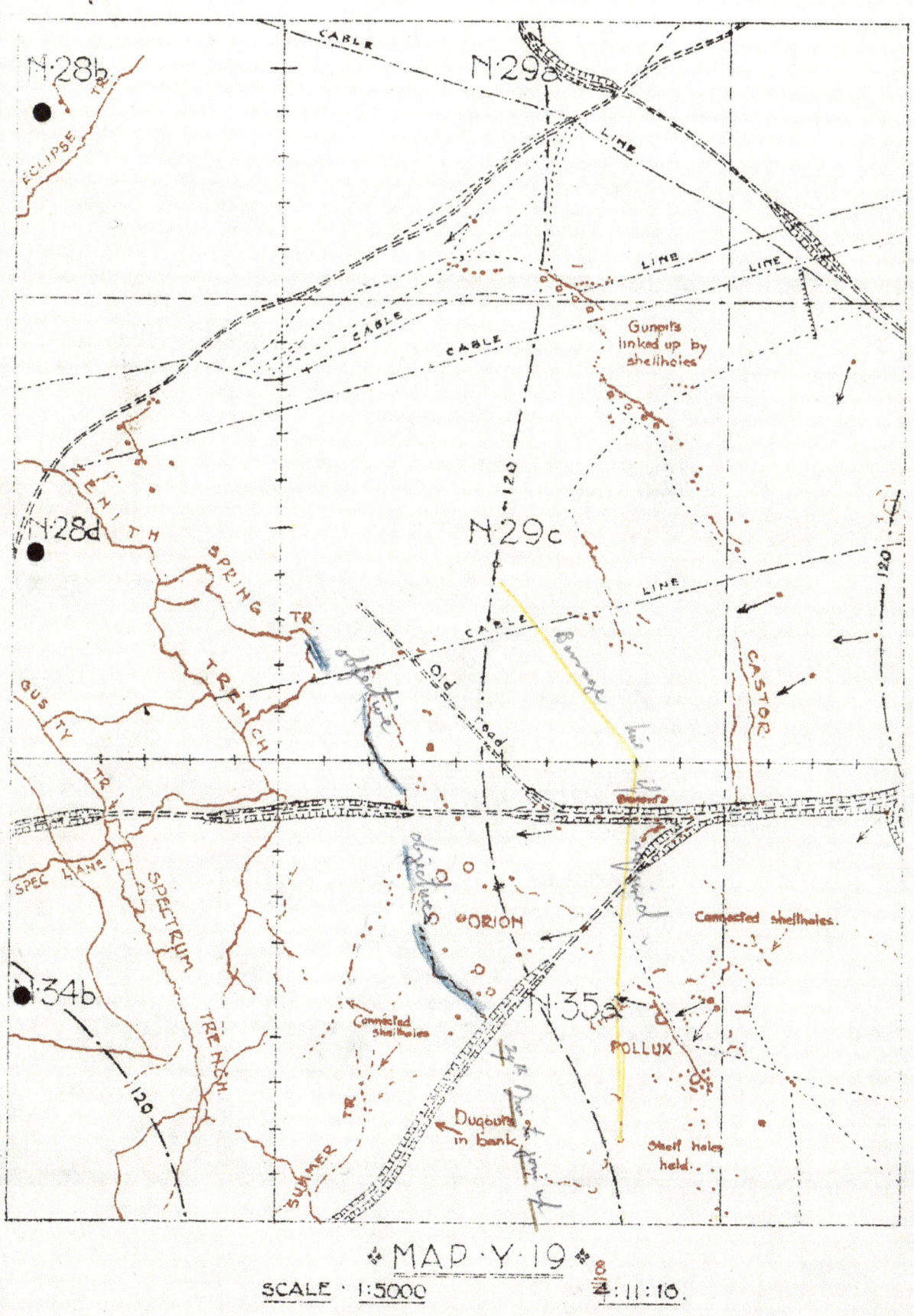

S E C R E T.　　　　　　　　　　　　　　　　　　　　Copy No. 11.

Warning Order.

1st Guards Brigade Order No. 90.

16th November 1916.

1. The Division will be relieved by 5th Australian Division probably on night of Nov: 21st/22nd.

2. On completion of relief Brigade will be disposed in the area - "H" Camp, CITADEL, SANDPITS, MEAULTE.

3. About Dec: 1st the Division will take over the SAILLY SAILLISEL Sector from the French.

ACKNOWLEDGE.

Captain,
Brigade Major, 1st Guards Brigade.

Copy No. 1 2nd Gren.Gds.,　　Copy No. 6 1st Guards T.M.Btty.,
   2 2nd Cold.Gds.,　　　　　　7 Bde., Transport Officer.
   3 3rd Cold.Gds.,　　　　　　8 Staff Captain.
   4 1st Irish Gds.,　　　　　　9 O.C., Signals.
   5 Bde.M.G.Coy.　　　　　　10, 11 & 12 Retained.

SECRET.   Copy No. 16

1st Guards Brigade Order No. 91.

Ref. Map - ALBERT 1/40,000.   Nov: 18th 1916.

1. The Right Group of Guards Division will be relieved by 8th Australian Infantry Brigade. Relief to be completed on the night of 21st/22nd Nov/

2. Units will move into the back area in accordance with Appendix "A" attached, which cancels the previous Roster of Reliefs issued from this Office on Nov: 15th.

3. Details of relief of front line Battalions and routes and times of starting of all Units will be issued later.

4. Work Platoons of Brigade will rejoin their Battalions on Nov: 21st, under Orders to be issued direct to the Platoons from this Office.

5. Defence Schemes, Secret Trench Sketches, Air Photographs, Schemes of Work and all Orders relating to the present Sector, will be handed over to relieving Units. Any of the above in possession of Units in the Camps will be sent to this Office before they move back.

6. 1st Line Transport will move in rear of Units. Times for movement of Transport of Units in the Line will be notified later.

7. Lorries are not available for the move.

8. Billeting parties will be sent in advance to take over Camps and will in each case report to the Camp Commandant who will allot accommodation.

9. (a) Gum boots will be handed over on relief.

   (b) A Dump will be made in Camp "H" under arrangements to be made by 1st Irish Guards, who will detail 1 N.C.O. and 3 men to take charge of this Store until the boots in it have been handed over to relieving Brigade.

   (c) Gum boots will be handed in to this Store as follows :-

   (i)   By 3/Cold.Gds. on morning of Nov:19th.
   (ii) " 2/Cold.Gds. during Nov:19th.
   (iii) " 1/Irish Gds.   "   "   "
   (iv) " 2/Gren.Gds.   "   "   20th.
   (v)   " 2/Irish Gds.   "   "   22nd.
   (vi) " 1/Cold.Gds.   "   "   "

- 2 -

    (d)   Units will wire this Office the numbers handed in and obtain receipts from the Storeman.

    (e)   Instructions for handing over these boots will be issued direct to Storeman from this Office.

10.   All Tools and S.A.A., will be dumped in Camp "H". Further details concerning this will be issued under a separate Order.

11.   Brigade H.Q., will close at WATERLOT FARM and open at the SANDPITS on completion of relief.

    ACKNOWLEDGE.

                                                  Captain,

    Brigade Major, 1st Guards Brigade.

Issued at :- 8.30 p.m.

Copy No.		Copy No.	
1	2nd Grenadier Guards.	9	Guards Division.
2	2nd Coldstream Guards.	10	2nd Guards Bde.,
3	3rd Coldstream Guards.	11	3rd Guards Brigade.
4	1st Irish Guards.	12	88th Inf. Bde.,
5	1st Coldstream Guards.	13	75th Field Coy. R.E.
6	2nd Irish Guards.	14	Right Group.
7	Bde., Machine Gun Company.	15	8th Australian Inf. Bde.,
8	1st Guards T.M. Battery.	16, 17 & 18	Retained.
		19.	Staff Capt.
		20.	Signals

APPENDIX 'A'.

MOVEMENTS OF GUARDS BRIGADES DURING RELIEF.

DATE	IN THE LINE	A & B CAMPS	D CAMP	F CAMP	H CAMP	MANSEL CAMP	CITADEL	SANDPITS	MEAULTE
19th.	2/Gren.Gds. to H Camp. 2 Coys. 1/Welsh Gds. to H Camp.	2/Irish Gds. to Line.	2 Coys. 1/Scots Gds. to Line. 1/Scots Gds. (less 2 Coys.) to H Camp.		3/Gren.Gds. to SANDPITS. 4/Gren.Gds. to SANDPITS.				
20th.	2 Coys. 1/Scots Gds. 1/Welsh Gds. (less 2 Coys.) to H Camp. 1/Gren.Gds. to F Camp. 3rd Bde.H.G. Coy.and 3rd Bde.T.M.Bty. to F Camp.			2/Scots Gds. to SANDPITS.	1/Irish Gds. to SANDPITS.				
21st.	3rd Gds.Bde. Hd.Qrs. to MEAULTE. 2/Irish Gds. 1/Coldstream Gds. to H Camp.			1/Gren.Gds. to MEAULTE. 3rd Gds.Bde. H.G.Coy. & T.M.Bty. to MEAULTE.	2/Gren.Gds. to MEAULTE. 1/Welsh Gds. to MEAULTE.	2/Cold:Gds. to MEAULTE. 3/Gren.Gds. to CITADEL. 2nd Gds.Bde. Hd.Qrs. to CITADEL. 2nd Gds.Bde. M.G.Coy. & T.M.Bty. to CITADEL.			
22nd.	1st Gds.Bde. Hd.Qrs. to SANDPITS.			1st Gds.Bde. M.G.Coy. & T.M.Bty. to SANDPITS.					

APPENDIX "B".

DISTRIBUTION ON COMPLETION OF RELIEF.

"H". CAMP	CITADEL.	SANDPITS.	MEAULTE.
1st Bn:Coldstream Guards. 1st Bn: Scots Guards. 2nd Bn: Irish Guards.	2nd Guards Bde.Hd.Qrs. " " M.G.Coy. " " T.M.Bty. 3rd Bn:Grenadier Guards. 4th Bn:Coldstream Guards. (PIONEERS). 1 Field Company, R.E. 1 -do- Ambulance.	1st Guards Bde.Hd.Qrs. " " M.G.Coy. " " T.M.Bty. 3rd Bn:Coldstream Guards. 1st Bn: Irish Guards. 4th Bn: Grenadier Guards. 2nd Bn: Scots Guards. 1 Field Company, R.E. 1 -do- Ambulance.	3rd Guards Bde.Hd.Qrs. " " M.G.Coy. " " T.M.Bty. 2nd Bn:Grenadier Guards. 2nd Bn: Coldstream Guards. 1st Bn: Grenadier Guards. 1st Bn: Welsh Guards. 1 Field Company, R.E. 1 -do- Ambulance.

Divisional Head Quarters
TREUX.

NOTE.- Accommodation for 3 Field Companies and Pioneer Battalion as shewn above is available, but it will depend on requirements of labour for hutting what proportion of R.E. remains in forward area.

SECRET.

2nd Bn. Grenadier Guards.
2nd Bn. Coldstream Guards.
3rd Bn. Coldstream Guards.
1st Bn. Irish Guards.
1st Bn. Coldstream Guards.
2nd Bn. Irish Guards.
Bde., Machine Gun Company.
1st Guards T. M. Battery.

Reference 1st Guards Brigade Order No. 21 issued to you last night, herewith appendix "B" which is to be attached.

19th Nov: 1915.

Captain,
Brigade Major, 1st Guards Bde.,

1. Any Units not shown in following Tables march under Brigade arrangements in accordance with Guards Division Order No. 95 (Appendix A).

DATE	UNIT	FROM	TO	ROUTE	REMARKS
19th.	3rd Bn. Coldstream Guards	H Camp	SANDPITS	CARNOY - road junction at F.18.c - FRICOURT Cemetery - CA.@AILLOT FAR.	Clears CARNOY 12.45 p.m.
	4th Bn. Grenadier Guards	H Camp	SANDPITS	-do-	Clears CARNOY 12 noon.
	2nd Bn. Scots Guards	F Camp	SANDPITS	CARNOY - road junction at F.18.c - FRICOURT Cemetery.	Starts 11.30 a.m.
20th.	1st Bn. Irish Guards	H Camp	SANDPITS	-do-	Starts 11 a.m.
	2nd Bn. Coldstream Guards	HANSEL CAMP.	MEAULTE	FRICOURT Cemetery.	Starts 8 a.m. Head of transport to pass road junction at S.27.c at 11 a.m. - thence by CARNOY - road junction at F.18.c.
	3rd Bn. Grenadier Guards	-do-	CITADEL	-do- Cookers with unit	Starts 8.30 a.m. Head of transport to pass road junction at S.27.c. at 11.10 a.m. Cookers with unit.
21st.	1st Bn. Welsh Guards	H Camp	MEAULTE	CARNOY - road junction at F.18.c - FRICOURT Cemetery.	Starts 9 a.m. Head of transport to pass road junction at S.27.c at 11.20 a.m. Cookers with unit
	2nd Bn. Grenadier Guards	H Camp	MEAULTE	-do-	Starts 9.30 a.m. Head of transport to pass road junction at S.27.c. at 11.30 a.m.
	1st Bn. Grenadier Guards.	F Camp	MEAULTE	-do-	Starts 10 a.m. Head of transport to pass road junction at S.27.c at 11.40 a.m. Cookers with unit.
	3rd Guards Bde M.G.Coy. 3rd Guards Bde T.M.Bty.	F Camp	MEAULTE	-do-	Starts 10.30 a.m. Head of transport to pass road junction at S.27.c at 11.50 a.m.
	55th Field Coy.R.E. 75th Field Coy. R.E. 76th Field Coy. R.E.	WATERLOT FARM. LONGUEVAL			Under arrangements of C.R.E. Not to start before 11 a.m.

2.

UNIT	FROM	TO	ROUTE	REMARKS
1st Guards Bde.M.G.Coy. 1st Guards Bde.T.M.Bty.	F Camp	SANDPITS.	CARNOY - road junction at F.18.c. - FRICOURT Cemetery.	Starts at 11 a.m.
Pioneer Bn.	TALMAS FARM. 1 Coy. from Camp F.	CITADEL. CITADEL.	BERNAFAY CORNER - OOSY CORNER - CARNOY - road junction at F.18.c. - FRICOURT Cemetery.	Starts 11 a.m. Follows in rear.

NOTE. MARCHING ORDER ON ROADS.

Troops marching along any roads East of the MEAULTE - ETINEHEM road will invariably march in file - with 200 yards interval between Companies.

This order also applies to the whole of the village of MEAULTE.

************* *************

SECRET.   Copy No. 14

Supplement to 1st Guards Bde. Order No. 91.

                                                  Nov: 19th, 1916.

1. (a) The 1st Bn. Coldstream Gds. will be relieved by 31st Australian Battn. on the night of Nov: 21st/22nd.

   (b) O.C. 31st Australian Battn. will be at H.Q. 2nd Irish Gds. at 12 noon tomorrow, 20th inst., 1st Coldstream Gds. will send a guide to be at H.Q. 2nd Irish Gds. by that hour.

   (c) On Nov: 21st, two front line Coy's. of 31st Australian Battn. will pass Brigade H.Q. at 3-30 P.M. The Support and Reserve Coy's. will pass Brigade H.Q. at 4-30 P.M.

   (d) Further details concerning guides etc. will be arranged direct between O.C's. concerned.

   (e) On completion of relief 1st Coldstream Gds. will proceed to Camp "H".

2. (a) The 2nd Bn. Irish Gds. will be relieved by 32nd Australian Battn. on the night of Nov: 21st/22nd.

   (b) O.C. 32nd Australian Battn. will be at H.Q. 2nd Irish Gds. at 12 noon tomorrow, 20th inst.,

   (c) On Nov: 21st, two front line Coy's. of 32nd Australian Battn. will pass Brigade H.Q. at 4 P.M. The Support and Reserve Coy's. will pass Brigade H.Q. at 5 P.M.

   (d) Further details concerning guides etc. will be arranged direct between O.C's. concerned.

   (e) On completion of relief 2nd Irish Gds. will proceed to Camp "H".

3. (a) The relief of Bde. Machine Gun Companies will be arranged direct between O.C. Bde. M.G.Companies but 8th Australian M.G. Company will not pass Brigade H.Q. before 6 P.M. on Nov: 21st.

   (b) O.C. 8th Australian M.G.Company will visit 1st Guards Bde. M.G.Company H.Q., tomorrow.

   (c) Gum boots of Bde. M.G.Company will be handed over direct to 8th Australian M.G.Company.

4. (a) 1st Guards Bde. Trench Mortar Battery will remain in it's present position until 22nd inst., when it will move to the SANDPITS in accordance with APPENDIX "B" of 1st Guards Bde. Order No. 91.

   (b) Two G.S.Wagons will be at "H" Camp on CARNOY - MONTAUBAN Road at 10 A.M. on 22nd inst.,

   (c) Gum boots of T.M.Battery will be handed into the Store in "H" Camp (see para.9 of Order No.91) during Nov:20th.

5.   Brigade H.Q., will close at WATERLOT Farm and open at the SANDPITS at 10 A.M. on Nov: 22nd, but all correspondence in envelopes from Battn's. in the back area should be sent to Brigade H.Q., Camp at the SANDPITS after 6 P.M. on Nov: 21st.

   ACKNOWLEDGE.

                                                      Captain,
                                    Brigade Major, 1st Guards Brigade.

- 2 -

Issued through Signals at :- 9·30 p.m.

Copy No. 1 2nd Bn. Grenadier Guards.
       2 2nd Bn. Coldstream Guards.
       3 3rd Bn. Coldstream Guards.
       4 1st Bn. Irish Guards.
       5 1st Bn. Coldstream Guards.
       6 2nd Bn. Irish Guards.
       7 Bde., Machine Gun Company.
       8 1st Guards T. M. Battery.
       9 8th Australian Inf. Bde.,
     10 2nd Guards Brigade.
     11 Staff Captain.
     12 O.C., Signals.
     13, 14, 15 & 16 Retained.

1st G.B. No.523/5.

O.C., Work Platoon of 2nd Grenadier Guards.
"   "   "   2nd Coldstream Guards.
"   "   "   3rd Coldstream Guards.
"   "   "   1st Irish Guards.
"   "   "   1st Coldstream Guards.
"   "   "   2nd Irish Guards.
2nd Guards Brigade (for information).

1. The attached Instructions to Work Platoons to rejoin their Battalions are issued.

2. All Troops will march in file.

3. All bivouacs will be handed over to Field Coy., relieving 75th Field Coy., R.E.

4. *Gum boots will be handed in to these H.Q. before moving off.* M.B.Smith

Captain,
20th Nov: 1916.
Brigade Major, 1st Guards Bde.,

INSTRUCTIONS 'RE' WORK PLATOONS RE-JOINING THEIR BATTALIONS.

Date.	Work Platoon.	Starting Point.	Time.	Route.	Destination.	Remarks.
Nov:21st.	2/Gren.Gds.	Present Bivouacs.	11-30 A.M.	CARNOY rd.junc. F.18.c. FRICOURT CEMETERY Le-CARCAILLOT.	MEAULTE.	Two G.S.Wagons will be at WATERLOT Farm at 10 AM. for blankets etc. of these 4 platoons. One wagon to go to MEAULTE & one to SANDPITS Camp.
"	2/Cold.Gds.	"	11-30 AM.	"	MEAULTE.	"
"	3/Cold.Gds.	"	11-35 AM.	"	SANDPITS E.29.d.	"
"	1/Irish Gds.	"	11-35 AM.	"	SANDPITS E.29.d.	"
"	1/Cold.Gds.	"	2 P.M.	MONTAUBAN.	Camp "H" A.8.a.8.2.	Transport arrangements to be made direct with Battn. Transport Officer.
"	2/Irish Gds.	"	2 P.M.	MONTAUBAN.	Camp "H".	"

SECRET.   Copy No. 9.

Warning Order
1st Guards Brigade Order No. 92.

November 25th, 1916.

Ref. Map - 57C. S.W. 1/20,000.

1. The Right Brigade Group will relieve the 114th French Infantry Regiment with one Battn., in the Line on the night of December 3rd.

2. The front held by 114th Regiment is from U.8.a.8.3. to U.1.d.8.3.

3. The 20th French Corps will be on the right and the 3rd Guards Brigade Left Group on the left.

4. Boundaries will be as follows :-

    Right Boundary. U.8.a.8.3. - U.8.a.0.1. - U.7.d.0.5. - road at U.13.a.0.7. thence to T.18.d.0.1. - thence in a straight line to N of STATION in T.29.a.

    Left Boundary. U.1.d.8.3. - U.7.b.0.8. - U.7.a.1.0. - T.18.a.0.0. - T.22.b.2.0. - Road junction T.27.b.8.3.

5. Movements into the Area will probably take place as follows :-

    Dec: 2nd. 3rd Coldstream Guards from SANDPITS to MALTZHORN FARM.

    Dec: 3rd. 3rd Coldstream Guards into Line.
    1st Irish Guards from SANDPITS Camp to COMBLES Area or MALTZHORN FARM.
    2nd Coldstream Guards to MALTZHORN FARM or COMBLES Area.
    2nd Grenadier Guards to BRONFAY FARM (F.29.a.)

"§"
6. Right Group Headquarters will be in the COMBLES CATACOMBS.

7. 1st Guards Bde. Machine Gun Company and Trench Mortar Battery will not move into the line until Dec: 6th/7th, when they will move into the Left Group Sector.

8. 1st Guards Brigade H.Q., will be in Reserve, position not yet known, until Dec: 10th/11th, when they will move to Right Group H.Q.,

    ACKNOWLEDGE.

                                                    Captain,
                                       Brigade Major, 1st Guards Brigade.

Issued at :- 8.30 p.m.

Copy No. 1 2nd Bn. Grenadier Guards. Copy No. 5 Bde. Machine Gun Company.
         2 2nd Bn. Coldstream Guards.   6 1st Guards T. M. Battery.
         3 3rd Bn. Coldstream Guards.   7 Staff Captain.
         4 1st Bn. Irish Guards.   8, 9 & 10 Retained.

"§" = Another Battn., frontage further South will be taken over soon after December 4th.

2nd Guards Brigade Operation
Orders

SECRET   Copy No. 11

Operation Order No. 77
by
Brigadier-General Lord H.C. Seymour, D.S.O.
Commanding 2nd. Guards Brigade.

-:*:-

27/11/16

WARNING ORDER
-:*:*:*:*:*:-

Right Guards Brigade Group will on the night of 7th/8th. December extend its right as far as U.14.b.9.6., relieving portion of 20th. French Corps.

1st. Bn. Irish Guards will carry out this relief, details of which, as well as of boundaries, etc., will be notified later.

ACKNOWLEDGE

H. L. Aubrey-Fletcher

Captain.
A/Brigade Major.

Copies to :-

No. 1 2nd. Bn. Grenadier Guards
No. 2 3rd. Bn. Grenadier Guards (For information)
No. 3 1st. Bn. Coldstream Guards
No. 4 2nd. Bn. Coldstream Guards
No. 5 3rd. Bn. Coldstream Guards
No. 6 1st. Bn. Scots Guards (For information)
No. 7 1st. Bn. Irish Guards
No. 8 2nd. Bn. Irish Guards
No. 9 2nd. Gds. Bde. M.G. Company
No.10 2nd. Gds. T.M. Battery
No.11 1st. Gds. Bde. (For information)
No.12 Guards Division (For information)
No.13 No.2 Coy Gds. Divl. Train
No.14 No. 4 Coy Gds. Divl. Train
No.15 2nd. Gds. Bde. Transport Officer
No.16 2nd. Guards Bde. Supply Officer
No.17 2nd. Gds. Bde. Signal Officer
No.18 Staff Captain.
No.19 War Diary
No.20 Office.

-:*:-

DEFENCE SCHEME

SCHEME OF WORK
ROSTER OF RELIEFS
HANDING OVER NOTES

S E C R E T.   1st G.B. No. 523/4

2nd Bn. Grenadier Guards.   1st Guards T. M. Battery.
2nd Bn. Coldstream Guards.   75th Field Coy., R.E.
3rd Bn. Coldstream Guards.   Right Group.
1st Bn. Irish Guards.   Guards Division.
Bde., Machine Gun Company.   3rd Guards Brigade.
1st Bn. Coldstream Guards.   88th Infantry Brigade.
2nd Bn. Irish Guards.

Herewith Defence Scheme for present Sector.

This Scheme will only be handed over when the Division is relieved.

Please acknowledge receipt.

[signature]

Captain,

17th November 1916.   Brigade Major, 1st Guards Brigade.

SECRET.

DEFENCE SCHEME

for Right Group of Guards Division.

17th November 1916.

FRONTAGE.

1. The frontage of the Brigade extends from N.34.b.7.3 to N.28.b.1.3.

BOUNDARIES.

2.
   (a) On the right - N.34.b.7.3 - road junction N.34.c.1.9 - road junction N.33.d.7.4. - cross roads T.3.a.9.8. - T.8.a.9 1/2.5.

   (b) On the left - N.28.b.1.3 - N.28.c.0.7 - N.33.b.0.7 - N.33.a.6.0 - N.32.d.8.2 - T.2.central - T.8.a.1.6.

METHOD OF HOLDING THE LINE.

3.
   (a) At present the line is held by two Battalions in the front line.
   Dividing line between these Battalions is - N.29.c.1.1 - cross roads N.34.a.1.9 - N.33.d.0.6 - N.33.c.0.0.

   Battn., H.Q., of Right Battn., are at road junc. N.34.a.3.0.

   Battn., H.Q., of Left Battn., are at N.33.c.1.1.

   (b) There is one Battalion in Support in Camp "A" TRONES WOOD. As soon as accommodation permits this Battn., will be moved up to hold the NEEDLE - COW Trench Line and the FLERS Line.

   (c) There is one Battalion in Reserve in "H" Camp (1)

   (d) The remaining Battalions of the Group and the M.G. Company and T.M. Battery out of the line form part of the Div. Reserve and will come under the orders of the Brigadier in Reserve at MANSEL Camp.

LINES OF DEFENCE.

4. There is no complete trench system in the Area but it is sub-divided as follows :-

   (a) Front Line system of fire and Support trenches which consist of SPRING and ZENITH as fire trenches - SPECTRUM and GUSTY as Support trenches. These trenches are not joined up and the only communication trench from front to rear is between SPRING and ZENITH at the S. end of the former.

   (b) Reserve Line - This should follow the line of ROSE trench but owing to the bad state of this line it is now only held by 1 platoon, the remainder being defended by Machine Guns.

   (c) The Intermediate Line, or COW Trench - NEEDLE Trench line.

   (d) The 2nd Line on the site of the FLERS Line.

MACHINE GUNS.

5. There are 6 Machine Guns in the front line - 6 in the Reserve Line - 2 in NEEDLE Trench Line and 2 in the FLERS Line.

ARTILLERY/

ARTILLERY.

6.   (a) The Group is supported by Right Group of Left Artillery XIV Corps.

      (b) H.Q., Right Group are at T.25.a.8.5.

      (c) Each Battalion in the front line will be in direct communication with a Battery.

      (d) "S.O.S". Lines on the Group Front are as follows :-
N.35.a.3.6 - N.29.c.4.3 - N.28.b.4 1/2.8.

      (e) One Observation Post on the front of each Battn. holding front line will be manned both by day and by night.

PRINCIPLES OF DEFENCE.

7. The following principles will be adopted in holding the line :-

      (a) The front line will be held as thinly as is consistent with security. To permit of thus holding the front line, good wire entanglements are necessary, good arrangements for flank defence, and close and continuous observation on the part of the Artillery F.O.O's.

      (b) Troops will NOT fall back from one line to any other line, but all ground will be defended as long as possible whether the flanks are turned or not.

      (c) There are three kinds of attack which may be anticipated :-

         (i) A raid.
         (ii) An attack on a minor scale to capture some locality, accompanied by a bombardment.
         (iii) A serious attack preceded by a heavy bombardment.

      (d) As regards (c) (1) :- Vigilance, active patrolling, combined with a good system of listening posts and wire, make the failure of such attacks certain.

      (e) As regards (c) (ii):- Should the enemy succeed in establishing himself in our trenches, he should be counter-attacked immediately from both flanks and from the Support trenches where such are in sufficiently close proximity.

The extent and intensity of the enemy's bombardment if closely observed, should give an indication of his objective and enable preparations for counter attack to be made before his attack is delivered. The essential is to deny him time in which to consolidate.

Should the counter attack fail, the captured portion of our trenches must be isolated by blocking, and Support trenches firmly held until more deliberate preparations can be made.

Meanwhile, the Artillery will prevent German reinforcements crossing "No Man's Land", and the Infantry must do their utmost to reconnoitre and locate the exact position held by the enemy, so that our Artillery may bombard the captured trenches with precision; thus, further counter attack by our Reserves will be executed under the most favourable conditions. Artillery fire will not be opened on the captured trenches without the sanction of the Guards Brigadier concerned.

      (f) As regards (c) (iii) :- It is unlikely that such an attack will come as a surprise, and Commanders will have time to make suitable dispositions.
In any case, no good will be gained by reinforcing the front line.

Supporting/

Supporting troops must hold their ground, and by means of fire and local attacks keep the enemy in check until sufficient Reserves are available to assume the offensive.

(g) All Officers must consider the action to be taken by the troops under their Command in the event of attack on any portion of the front for the defence of which they are responsible. Plans must be thought out beforehand, and the action to be taken known to all. Nothing should be left to chance.
Battalions and Companies must keep each other informed of their plans to meet various eventualities.

Action by Battn's. in Support
& Reserve in event of Attack.

8. (a) The Battn. in Camp "A" will be prepared to move on receupt of Orders and garrison COW and NEEDLE Trenches in the Brigade Area with 2 Coys. and the FLERS Line in the Bde. Area with 2 Coys.

(b) The Battn. in Camp "H" will be prepared on receipt of Orders to move to Camp "A".

(c) If ordered to move these Battn's. will at once each send an Officer to report at Brigade H.Q.,

(d) All movement over the GINCHY - DELVILLE WOOD crest and the T.8.a. crest will be as far as possible by communication trenches. Commdg., Officers and Company Commdrs., must reconnoitre the ground over which their Units may have to pass.

(e) 75th Field Coy., R.E., T.M.Battery, and Work Platoons will 'Stand To' in their billets ready to move at shortbnotice.

"S.O.S". SIGNAL.

9. The "S.O.S" Signal is five RED Rockets bursting into GREEN, fired in rapid succession. This means that the enemy has actually been seen leaving his trenches.

GAS ATTACK.

10. In case of a "GAS ATTACK", the alarm will be spread by every available means.
Telephone Operators will send "GAS" to all concerned.
Infantry, Lewis Guns, and Machine Guns will open steady regulated fire on the German trenches.
Artillery will open a deliberate fire on the German trenches and get ready for rapid barrage in case of receipt of "S.O.S" message, or on seeing the "S.O.S" Rocket Signal.

NOTE. In spreading the alarm for Gas Shell bombardments, Strombus Horns, Gongs, and other Signals for a Gas Attack will not be employed.

Captain.

Brigade Major, 1st Guards Brigade.

2nd Bn. Grenadier Guards.　　1st Bn. Coldstream Guards.
2nd Bn. Coldstream Guards.　　2nd Bn. Irish Guards.
3rd Bn. Coldstream Guards.　　2nd Guards Brigade.
1st Bn. Irish Guards.　　　　　Guards Division.
Bde., Machine Gun Company.　　75th Field Coy., R.E.
1st Guards T. M. Battery.　　　Staff Captain.

General Scheme of Work in Right Group of Guards Division.

1. The scheme of work to be carried out by Battalions in the front line will be as follows :-

(a) <u>Front line Coys.</u> will be employed on -

　(1) Making the front and support lines i.e. SPRING - ZENITH - SPECTRUM continuous and joining up front and support lines by good communication trenches.

　(2) Wiring front line.

　(3)

(b) <u>Support Coys.</u>

　(1) Each Battalion in the front line will detail 1 Officer and 50 men nightly for work under 75th Field Coy., R.E. on WINDMILL Lane. R.E. will report at Battn., H.Q., at 6 P.M. nightly for these parties.
　Parties to bring shovels and mud scoops.
　On relief nights outgoing Battalions will detail these parties which will return to Camp on completion of their task.

(c) When communication trenches between firing line and support are complete a communication trench back from the support line to join up with WINDMILL Lane in right sub-sector and SHRINE Alley in left sub-sector will be started.

(d) The wiring of NEEDLE and COW Trenches will be put in hand at once by the garrison.

(e) Burial of dead must be carried on.

2. R.E.
　(a) Two sections on dug-outs for new Battn., H.Q., in COW and WINDMILL Trench.

　(b) 1 section on reclaiming WINDMILL Trench as a communication trench.

　(c) 1 section on Machine Gun dug-outs, labour to be supplied by Machine Gun Company.

3. WORK PLATOONS.

　Will be employed under R.E., All 6 platoons will eventually be employed in the forward area and be billeted near Brigade H.Q., They will be employed on carrying and on the Tunnel dug-outs in COW and WINDMILL Trench.

4. T. M. BATTERY.

　Will be employed for carrying purposes.

- 2 -

5. **MULES.**

    All mules of Battalions in the Group will be Brigaded. As many as are required will always be allotted to the Battalions in and to the Battalions going into the front line for rations and water. The mules of an incoming Battalion will be available for use by the outgoing Battalion.
    The Staff Captain is responsible for the allotment of remaining mule transport and carrying parties. Units requiring any of these will wire their requirements as early as possible to the Staff Captain, who will then detail convoys accordingly.

6. **R. E. MATERIAL.**

    All R.E. material required by Battalions in the front line can be drawn from the Brigade Store in T. 8. Central. Battalions will wire every morning what they require to draw that night. They will then be informed whether the material can be delivered or whether they will have to draw themselves. Every effort will be made to deliver to Battalions in the line. Battalions are responsible that sufficient material for carrying on the work in hand for 24 hours is handed over to relieving Battalions.

7. **BOMB STORE.**

    The Brigade Bomb Store is also at T. 8. Central and requirements of this sort will be dealt with in the same way as for R.E. material (see above).

8. **SALVAGE.**

    Every effort must be made to use the returning parties, individuals or mules for taking back Salvage and empty petrol tins either to the 1st Line Transport - to the Brigade Dump at T. 8. Central, or to Brigade H.Q.,
    Company and Battalion Dumps must be formed.

9. **DUCK BOARDS.**

    Mules are not allowed to walk along the duck boards. The best way up for mules is through GUILLEMONT and GINCHY - thence down FLERS Road until the white tape is struck - thence down the tape to Battalion H.Q.,
    The white tape will be moved under Brigade arrangements from time to time so as to prevent the track becoming too cut up.

10. **RETURNS.**

    The following reports are required by Battalions in the line :-

    Morning situation report, by wire   - 4 A.M.

    Intelligence report, by first orderly   - 11 A.M.
    Under headings -
    A. Enemy defences, work, etc.,
    B. Movements in enemy lines and in rear on tracks at dumps, etc.,
    C. Signalling, lights used by enemy.
    D. Gas.
    E. Miscellaneous.
    F. Work, and number of coils of wire put out.

    Above to cover as nearly as possible a period from 8-30 A.M. to 8-30 A.M.

    Evening situation report, by wire   - 4 P.M.
    Casualty report by wire in code   - 5 P.M.
    Casualty report will be rendered by all Battn's. in the Group DAILY to their own Bde. H.Q. repeating them to the Group H.Q. for information.

11/

11. OBSERVATION POSTS.

Must be established along the front so as to have the whole of the enemy's front opposite us under observation.
Sniping and Intelligence will be carried on under the usual Brigade arrangements.

12. TRENCH BOARDS.

As many trench boards as possible will be sent up daily to Battalions in the front line – to be used for boarding the firing line and support trenches and communication trenches between them.

13. SANDBAGS.

Every man going into the trenches will take up 4 sandbags.

14. TRANSPORT.

The quickest way up for Transport from the present Transport Lines is via CARNOY and MARICOURT.

15. STRETCHER BEARERS.

Will be made up to 32 per Battalion.

16. TUNNELLING COY.

It is hoped that a Tunnelling Coy., will shortly be employed in the Sector.

17. CAMPS.

Plans for improvements to Camps will be made out as follows and forwarded to this Office :-

By O.C., 3/Cold.Gds. for "H" Camp 1.
" O.C., 1/Irish Gds.for "H" Camp 2.
" O.C., 2/Irish Gds.for MANSELL CAMP.
" O.C., 1/Cold.Gds. for Camp "A".

As soon as a plan has been decided upon it is hoped with the concurrence of Battalions to make a Battn. Pioneer Sgt. responsible for the execution of the plan.
This Sgt. would remain for the whole tour with a nucleus of his Battn. Pioneers in the Camp for which he was responsible and would call on the Battn. in the Camp for any labour he required.
In the same way, two Pioneer Sgt's. and a nucleus would be allotted to the Bde., Transport Officer.
Plans for Camps as above to reach this Office by 8 P.M. 16th inst.,

15th November 1916.

Captain,
Brigade Major, 1st Guards Bde.,

SECRET.

2nd Bn. Grenadier Guards.	1st Guards T. M. Battery.
2nd Bn. Coldstream Guards.	1st Bn. Coldstream Guards.
3rd Bn. Coldstream Guards.	2nd Bn. Irish Guards.
1st Bn. Irish Guards.	2nd Guards Brigade.
Bde., Machine Gun Company.	Guards Division.

1. (a) Herewith Roster of Reliefs in Right Brigade Group from Nov: 15th to 20th inclusive.

   (b) After Nov: 20th the Roster will run on in the same way, if the tresent one works satisfactorily.

   (c) A Roster for Nov: 20th to 28th will be issued about Nov: 18th.

2. Relief of Battn's in the front line will be arranged direct between Battn's concerned.

3. Battn's. moving into the line from Camp "A" will notify this Office of the time and route by which the relief is to be carried out.

4. Battn's. moving into any Camp will always send a billeting party to take over that Camp at 2 P.M. on the day on which it starts to move.
   This will enable the Camp to be taken over in daylight and permit of Stores being checked.
   Receipts for these Stores will be obtained and forwarded by the out-going Unit to this Office.

5. In the same way Battn's. moving into the front line will send on a party at a time to be arranged between Battn's. concerned on the day of relief. This party will take over Snipers Posts, Observation Posts, Trench Stores and Telephone Lines.

6. The Battn. at "H" Camp No. 2, and the Battn. at MANSELL Camp will be under the Orders of the Reserve Brigadier for tactical purposes - also the Machine Gun Company and Trench Mortar Battery in Reserve.

7. Units however will always be controlled by their own Brigadier for administrative purposes through the usual channels.

8. It is hoped shortly to issue a Scheme of Work for the period during which the Division will be in the line.
   Meanwhile Units will carry on the Scheme of Work handed over by 17th Division.

9. Every effort must be made by Battn's. in Camps to improve their Camps permanently, and particular attention must also be paid to the Transport Lines.

10. 1st Line Transport will not move with it's Unit after it has once reached the permanent Brigade Lines at A.2.b.6.2.

11. It is hoped to allot each Battn. a permanent Store Hut to put extra equipment in when it moves into the Line.

12th November 1916.

Captain,
Brigade Major, 1st Guards Brigade.

S E C R E T.   1st G.B. No.501.

2nd Bn. Grenadier Guards.   1st Guards T. M. Battery.
2nd Bn. Coldstream Guards.   1st Bn. Coldstream Guards.
3rd Bn. Coldstream Guards.   2nd Bn. Irish Guards.
1st Bn. Irish Guards.   2nd Guards Brigade.
Bde., Machine Gun Company.   Guards Division.

Reference this Office No.501 of the 15th inst.,

Herewith amended Roster of Reliefs.

The amendment is due to the 2nd Coldstream Guards having to carry out a minor operation on the night of 18/19th November, which necessitates the 2nd Coldstream Guards and 2nd Grenadier Guards having to do a tour of 3 days in the front line. After this, the tour of duty in the front line will be 48 hours.

18th November 1916.

Brigade Major, 1st Guards Brigade.
                                                 Captain,

Position of Components of Right Group Battalions of Guards Division.

	Front Line Right Batt., Left Batt.	Camp A & B TROIS WOOD B.3.d.6.8.	Camp II = A.9.c.0.9. No. 1 Camp.	No. 2 Camp.	MAGNILL CAMP.
Nov 15th	3/C.G. relieved by 2/C.G. & move to Camp H (a).	—	—		
" 16th	2/C.G.	1/C.G. relieved by 3/C.G. & move to Camp H (a).	3/C.G.		1/C.G. arrive.
" 17th	2/C.G.	3/C.G.	3/C.G.		1/C.G. move to Camp A.
" 18th	2/C.G. 1/C.G. relieved & move to MAGNILL Camp.	3/C.G.	3/C.G.		1/C.G.
" 19th	1/C.G.	3/C.G. 2/C.G. relieved & move to Camp H (a).	3/C.G. 2/C.G. move to Camp A.		
" 20th	1/C.G. relieved by 3/C.G. & move to Camp H (a).	3/C.G. 1/C.G. relieved	2/C.G.	1/C.G. move to Camp	2/B.G.
	1st Guards Bde., L.G. Company and 1st Guards Bde., H.Q. relieved by 2nd Guards Bde., H.Q. and Guards Reserve B.				
" 21st	3/C.G.	1/C.G. relieved by 1/I.G.	2/C.G.	1/C.G.	2/C.G. move to Camp A.

Handing over Notes on 1st Guards Brigade Sector.
----

1. The front line trenches in the Brigade Area are situated on the crest or just on the forward slope of a ridge which runs practically due North and South.

2. The Germans have no connected line of trenches nearer than the TRANSLOY Line, but they occupy a line of shell holes, connected in some places, and at a distance varying from 200 yards to 40 yards from our own front line. The chief of these on the Brigade front are known as FINCH and ORION Trenches. It is the Northern end of the former which is only 40 yards from our front line.

3. It is just at this point too where the junction of the right and left Battalions should be but at present there is a gap of about 30 yards between the two Battalions.

4. The front line is not continuous, nor do a quarter of their trenches marked on the Map exist. Those actually held are shown in thick red chalk on attached sketch. The only C.T. which exists runs from the Southern part of ZENITH through SPECTRUM and just back over the crest of the ridge. SPRING trench is joined to ZENITH at both ends by C.T's. which are almost as necessary for fire trenches as C.T's. There is a gap of 80 yards between our right Battn. and the left Battn. of the next Brigade (88th Infantry Brigade).

5. Behind the ridge on which our front trenches stand, runs a valley which the enemy cannot observe and which they search with shell fire continuously day and night. The cross roads named the MILLERS SON is the most dangerous point. A Valley runs from the present left Battn. H.Q. i.e. NEEDLE Dump down to the MILLERS SON and this too is constantly shelled as well as the ridge where SHIN ALLEY and WINDMILL LANE meet, but the enemy can only observe their fire on the top of the ridges and then only from some distance off, about BEAULENCOURT.

6. The condition of the trenches is fair but they require revetting and trench boarding especially the latter as in the wet they soon give way and become very muddy. Those that do exist are all deep but there are no dugouts of any sort. Parapets should on no account be undercut as they then immediately give way.

7. One of the greatest difficulties has been that of finding the way at night. There is absolutely no landmarks of any kind and reliefs and orderlies are always losing their way. Tapes, stakes and bicycle lamps have been used to try and rectify this and it is hoped that the difficulty has now been largely overcome. Apparently the enemy experience the same difficulty as every night one or more prisoners have been captured often behind our lines.

8. Owing to the difficulty of communication and the difficulty of getting any Stores up to the front line the following Scheme of Work is proposed and has been started on:-

(a) Complete Duck-boards as near up to front line as possible. At present these only reach to about one third of the way between the two Battn. H.Q. The best route for the completion of the line of duck-boards is shown on the attached sketch in dotted blue lines. It should aim at joining the C.T. which has already been dug in right Battn. Area from ZENITH through SPECTRUM and back over the crest on which our front trenches stand.

(b)/

- 2 -

(b) As soon as duck-board communication has been established, a communication trench should be started from front to rear following roughly the line of the duck-boards. As this communication trench is dug the duck-boards constituting the duck-board path should be laid in it, otherwise the labour of digging a C.T. will be wasted. If possible the C.T. should be dug when the ground is fairly dry.
Draining and revetting are almost as important as trench boarding.

(c) The right Battn. should start digging a C.T. from ZENITH through GUSTY to join up with the C.T. mentioned about N.34.a.5.6. shown in attached sketch thus

(d) The front line Coy's. should aim at :-

    (i)   Making line continuous.
    (ii) Getting communication to support line.
    (iii) Wiring.

(e) Support Coy's. should try and extend ~~outwards~~ ROSE trench to join up.

(f) Reserve Coy's. are available to help with above work - also for carrying up rations and material.

(g) Wiring if NEEDLE and COW trenches must be continued.

9.   Other Work in hand in the Area is as follows :-

(a) New Battn. H.Q. for both Battn. H.Q. - Right Battn. in WINDMILL trench - Left Battn. COW trench. This is being done by Tunnelling Coy.,

(b) Machine Gun emplacements and dugouts roughly on the line ROSE trench, also by Tunnelling Coy.,

(c) A new C.T. from a point about 300 yards E. of Brigade H.Q. to NEEDLE Dump is under construction by PIONEERS. It is in use over the GINCHY - DELVILLE WOOD crest and will shortly be ready for use over the crest where the old FLERS Line runs. It is essential that this trench be used over both crests when completed. At present the continuous hostile shelling is due to too much movement over the crests and down the slope from the FLERS Line to NEEDLE Dump. There is also too much movement about NEEDLE Dump and MAIL trench.

(d) The Pioneers have also been digging a C.T. to the left Brigade Area from NEEDLE Dump and have been working on WINDMILL LANE up to ROSE Trench.

MACHINE GUNS.

10.   There are six Machine Guns in the front line, all shooting over the parapet.
There are six on the line of ROSE Trench, two in the NEEDLE COW trench line and two in the old FLERS Line.

ARTILLERY.

11.   The front is covered by Right Group Left Artillery XIV Corps under Colonel Head. His H.Q. are on the South side of GUILLEMONT T. 26.a too far away.

Each Battalion in the line is in direct communication with a Battery and an O.P. but this requires improvement. An Artillery Officer visits Battn. H.Q. each day and an O.P. on each Battalion front is manned by night.

- 3 -

R.E. COMPANY.

12.   Billets of R.E. Company and Work Platoons are 150 yards West of Brigade H.Q.,

MULE TRACKS.

13.   A new track for mules has been completed and is as follows - GUILLEMONT - GINCHY - FLERS Road to the point where it crosses the old FLERS Line - thence right handed along a tape to NEEDLE Dump.
    This track should on no account go near the line of duck-boards. Permanent Police should live at Brigade Dump at T.8.a. central to keep stray mules off the duck-boards.

DUMPS of R.E. & BOMBS ETC.,

14.   Brigade Dumps are at T.8.a. central and at NEEDLE trench - All carrying by hand or by mule.

    There must be no movement of mules or carrying parties over the open East of the old FLERS Line.

Salvage

15.   Coys salvage as much as possible in their own areas & dump at Bde H.Q. Returning mules dump at Bde dumps or 1st line transport. It is suggested that the PIONEER Bn returning from work might do a good deal more salvage than at present.

H.Q., 1st Guards Bde.,
20th November 1916.

Captain,
Brigade Major, 1st Guards Bde.,

INTELLIGENCE

Headquarters,
Guards Division.

Intelligence Report.

A. Enemys line in front of Right Battalion appears to be a line of unconnected posts about 50 to 120 yds. apart with strong points in FINCH Trench and ORION Trench - The average distance of these from our front line is 100 yards. A patrol which went out from N.35.A.1.6 last night confirms the above and in addition states that in front of ZENITH Trench 2 snipers in front of the line of posts were located. The going in "No Man's Land" is now hard and good and free of shell holes.

B. A party of enemy moving about in front of SPRING Trench were fired on and one of them slightly wounded came in - Prisoner belongs to 28th ERSATZ Regiment.

15/11/1916.

Captain.
for Brigadier General.
Commanding 1st Guards Brigade.

Headquarters,
   Guards Division.

                  Intelligence Report.

A.   No new work in enemy's front line visible.

B.   Party of 50 men were seen digging West of
        LE TRANSLOY. Hostile snipers active at Northern
        end of FINCH Trench.

C.   Enemy appears to observe parties moving over
        the high ground in N.28.c. by means of Very Lights
        from the flank. A red light frequently produces
        a well directed salvo.

E.   Enemy shelled the whole of forward area
        continuously during last 24 hours, chiefly the
        ridges in N.28.c. - N.33.a. and c. - N.33.d.
        2nd Bn. Coldstream Guards relieved 3rd Bn. Coldstream
        Guards in right sub-sector. Some casualties owing
        to hostile shelling.

                                            Brigadier General,
16th November 1916.   Commdg., 1st Guards Brigade.

www.ingramcontent.com/pod-product-compliance
Lightning Source LLC
Chambersburg PA
CBHW081431160426
43193CB00013B/2248